Duden Schülerhilfen

Englisch 10. Klasse

Übungen zur Grammatik und zum Textverständnis

Duden Schülerhilfen

Duden Schülerhilfen

Englisch 10. Klasse

Übungen zur Grammatik
und zum Textverständnis

von Sylvia Böhm

mit Illustrationen von Detlef Surrey

Dudenverlag
Mannheim · Leipzig · Wien · Zürich

Die Deutsche Bibliothek – CIP-Einheitsaufnahme
Ein Titeldatensatz für diese Publikation
ist bei der Deutschen Bibliothek erhältlich.

Das Wort **Duden** ist für den Verlag
Bibliographisches Institut & F. A. Brockhaus AG
als Marke geschützt.

Das Werk wurde in neuer Rechtschreibung verfasst.
1. Auflage

Redaktionelle Leitung: Martin Fruhstorfer
Herstellung: Petra Schäffner
Redaktion: Linda Strehl
Korrektorat: Christine Schlitt
Satz: Atelier Frank Wohlgemuth, Bremen
Umschlaggestaltung: Bender & Büwendt, Berlin
Druck: Druckhaus Langenscheidt KG, Berlin
Gedruckt auf Eural Super Recyclingpapier mattgestrichen
Bindearbeit: Schöneberger Buchbinderei, Berlin
Printed in Germany
ISBN 3-411-71331-3

Liebe Schülerin, lieber Schüler,

das Ende der Mittelstufe rückt immer näher, und wir wollen dir in diesem Buch sichere Grundlagen für diese und die folgenden Klassen geben. Du kannst mit dem Buch zwei Ziele erreichen:

1. Wortschatz und Grammatik aus den zurückliegenden Unterrichtsjahren gezielt wiederholen und somit Lücken schließen,
2. dich auf Übungs- und Testformen vorbereiten, die in den folgenden Jahren von dir gefordert werden.

Was enthält dieses Buch?

- Ein großes Wiederholungskapitel – es zeigt dir, welchen Lernstoff du eventuell wiederholen solltest.
- Einführung und Vertiefung des “summary writing”.
- Sechs Texte mit Fragen zum Textverständnis. Du kannst hier die Testform “reading comprehension” üben. Im Anschluss an die Fragen zum jeweiligen Text findest du zahlreiche Fragen zu Wortschatz und Grammatik, die sich meist auf das im Text enthaltene Sprachmaterial beziehen. Dieser Übungsteil ermöglicht es dir, deinen Wortschatz zu erweitern und deine Grammatikkenntnisse zu vertiefen.
- Am Ende des Buches kannst du anhand von vier Texten das Übersetzen aus der Fremdsprache üben. Dies ist eine Testform, die in der Oberstufe eine wichtige Rolle spielt.

Wie arbeitest du mit diesem Buch?

Die Texte in den einzelnen Kapiteln weisen einen leicht steigenden Schwierigkeitsgrad auf, es wäre also gut, wenn du sie der Reihe nach bearbeitest.

Nimm dir nicht zu viel auf einmal vor, es ist besser, die Übungen öfter zu wiederholen.

Kontrolliere deine Antworten stets im Lösungsteil. Bei manchen Aufgaben, etwa zu den Zusammenfassungen, zum Textverständnis oder zur Übersetzung aus dem Englischen, können die Lösungen natürlich nur Musterlösungen sein. Wenn deine Lösungen nicht so ausführlich sind, so ist das nicht schlimm: Vergleiche sie mit den angegebenen und überlege, ob deine auch richtig sind und worin sie sich unterscheiden. Notiere die Musterlösungen der Sätze, in denen du Fehler gemacht hast, in einem Fehlerheft oder auf Karteikarten. Wiederhole die korrekten Lösungen öfters, insbesondere vor Klassenarbeiten.

Vorwort

Um dir bei der Arbeit die Übersicht zu erleichtern, gibt es die folgenden Zeichen:

Regel → 

Fehlerquelle → 

Tipp → 

Beispiel → 

Aufgabe → 

Und nun wünsche ich dir viel Freude bei der Arbeit mit diesem Buch und natürlich auch viel Erfolg.
In diesem Sinne: Pluck up your courage! You can do it!

Sylvia Böhm
Mannheim, im Frühjahr 2001

Wiederholung – Revision

Am Anfang des Buches steht ein Check-up, eine Überprüfung deiner Grundkenntnisse. Er soll dir helfen, deine individuellen Lernlücken aufzuspüren und sie Schritt für Schritt zu schließen.
Erfahrungsgemäß werden in der 10. Klasse die meisten Fehler im Bereich der Verbgrammatik gemacht. Daher liegt der Schwerpunkt des Check-ups auf der Bildung der Zeiten und ihrer korrekten Verwendung im Textzusammenhang.

Wie arbeitest du mit dem Check-up?
Der Check-up ist so aufgebaut, dass bestimmte Regeln und Erläuterungen immer wieder abgerufen werden. Ganz wichtig: Es reicht nicht, nur die gesuchte Lösung zu haben, sondern vor allem musst du erklären können, warum du dich für diese Lösung entschieden hast!
Du solltest die Lücken nicht im Buch ausfüllen, sondern die ganzen Antworten in ein Heft eintragen. So kannst du diesen Check-up ab und zu wiederholen, deine individuellen Lücken eingrenzen und somit gezielt angehen.
Im Lösungsteil findest du die Lösungen zu diesem Lückentext komplett zusammengestellt. Direkt nach dem Text werden diese Lösungen im Hinblick auf Besonderheiten und grammatische Schwierigkeiten näher beleuchtet. Die in Klammern stehenden Zahlen helfen dir beim Auffinden der Erläuterungen.

1.1 A Tour of London

Complete the following text. Put the verbs in brackets in the correct tense of the passive or active voice. Sometimes you may have to use a participle or gerund construction. Choose the right form of the adjectives and adverbs.

London ___is visited___ (1 – visit) by millions of tourists every year as it is one of the ___largest___ (2 – large) and ___most exciting___ (2 – exciting) cities in the world.

One of the sights that you can been see (3 – can/see) from the River Thames is London's landmark Big Ben. Big Ben is really the name which has been given (4 – give) to the huge bell inside the clock tower. The real name of the tower is St Stephen's Tower, by the way.

I'm sure you ________________ (4 – see) pictures of the building next to Big Ben before. The Houses of Parliament ________________ (5 – stand) on the site of the Royal Palace of Westminster. The Palace ________________ (6 – damage/very/bad) by fire in 1834 and all that ________________ (7 – can/save) was Westminster Hall, one of the ________________ (8 – fine) halls in Western Europe. A stone's throw away from Parliament there is Westminster Abbey. Since 1066, all English kings and queens ________________ (9 – crown) in this church. Many famous people ________________ (10 – bury – begraben) here. Westminster is also the name ________________ (11 – use) for a central London borough, which ________________ (12 – contain) several important buildings, ________________ (12 – include) Buckingham Palace, the London home of the Queen. If the flag ________________ (13 – fly) on top, it ________________ (14 – mean) she is at home.

Most tourists ________________ (15 – attract) by the Changing of the Guard, a ceremony ________________ (16 – hold) in the forecourt of the Palace every morning. The new guard,

_____________ (17 – lead) by a band, _______________________ (18 – arrive) to take over from the old guard.

___________________________ (19 – know/you) where the crown jewels ___________________________ (20 – keep)? Of course, in the Tower of London. Does anybody remember the name of a famous prisoner there? Right, the explorer Sir Walter Raleigh who was executed although he ________________________ (21 – fight) against the Spanish Armada.

From nearby Tower Bridge you ___________________________ (22 – can/easy/see) Canary Wharf Tower, Britain's tallest skyscraper. It is in the Docklands, where some old docks ____________________________ (23 – close down). Some years ago many poor families ___________ ____________ (24 – must) leave the area because they could no longer afford _______________________ (25 – live) in this rich neighbourhood

although they ______________________________

(26 – would/enjoy/stay) there. At the moment more and more flats ______________________________ (27 – build). If the former inhabitants ______________________ (28 – come) back in a couple of years, they ________________________ (29 – not recognize) their area any longer. It ______________________________ (30 – change/complete). An elderly lady recently said she ______________________ (31 – not want) to go back to the place because it ______________________ (31 – be) too sad for her.

1.

London **is visited**
London **wird besucht**

Die deutsche Übersetzung „wird besucht" könnte dazu verleiten, das Wort „wird" mit "will" oder "become" zu übersetzen. Das deutsche „wird" drückt hier jedoch das **Passiv** aus!

Im Englischen bildet man das Passiv mit einer Form des Hilfsverbs "be" (z. B. "am", "was") + past participle (z. B. "known", "seen").

Yesterday one of the Royals **was seen** at Harrod's.	Gestern **wurde** ein Mitglied der königlichen Familie bei Harrod's **gesehen.**

Die Passivkonstruktion wird im Fall von "is visited" zusätzlich durch die eigentlich handelnden Personen "by millions of tourists" markiert. Im Englischen verwendet man dafür den Ausdruck "by-agent". Das "by-agent" entfällt beim Passiv häufig, da aus dem Textzusammenhang meist hervorgeht, wer handelt.

Außerdem legt das Signalwort die Wahl des "aspect" fest, d.h. ob simple form oder progressive form zu verwenden ist: Mit "every" verbindet man eine regelmäßige, gewohnheitsmäßige Handlung, sodass "visit" in die simple form gesetzt werden muss. Würde anstelle von "every year" "this summer" stehen, müsste die progressive form gewählt werden, also: "London is being visited."

2.

one of the **largest** and **most exciting** cities
eine der **größten** und **aufregendsten** Städte

Die Fügung "one of the" macht deutlich, dass im Folgenden nur der **Superlativ** in Frage kommen kann. Bei den Steigerungsformen der Adjektive – man bezeichnet sie als comparative und superlative – unterscheidet man im Englischen zwei Gruppen: die Formen mit "-er/-est" und die mit "more/most".

Zur ersten Gruppe gehören:
– Adjektive mit einer Silbe wie
large – larg**er** – larg**est**
high – high**er** – high**est**
big – bigg**er** – bigg**est** (der Konsonant "g" wird verdoppelt, weil der vorausgehende Vokal kurz gesprochen wird)

– Adjektive mit zwei Silben, die auf "-er", "-le", "-ow" oder "-y" enden:
clever – clever**er** – clever**est**
simple – simpl**er** – simpl**est**
narrow – narrow**er** – narrow**est**
happy – happi**er** – happi**est** (hier wird "-y" nach Konsonant zu "-ie")

Zur zweiten Gruppe gehören alle zwei- und mehrsilbigen Adjektive, die nicht auf die genannten Silben enden:
basic – **more** basic – **most** basic
interesting – **more** interesting – **most** interesting

Beachte vor allem folgende unregelmäßige Formen, die häufig gebraucht werden:

good/well – better – best
bad/ill – worse – worst
little (klein) – smaller – smallest
little (wenig) – less – least
much/many – more – most

Regelmäßig wird jedoch "few" gebraucht:

few (wenige) – fewer – fewest

„Die meisten" entspricht im Englischen stets "most" ohne Artikel!
***Die meisten** Kinder lieben Pommes. – **Most** children love chips.*

Je mehr Adjektive du kennst, umso differenzierter kannst du Sachverhalte und Personen beschreiben. Das wirkt sich positiv für dein Punktekonto in der Rubrik „sprachliche Ausdrucksfähigkeit" aus!

3.

one of the sights that **can be seen** from the River Thames
eine der Sehenswürdigkeiten, die von der Themse aus **gesehen werden können**

Hier handelt es sich um eine **Passivkonstruktion mit einem Hilfsverb.** Sie folgt immer dem Muster: Hilfsverb + "be" + past participle.

Hilfsverben sind:

can – could – may – might – will – would – shall – should – must – need – ought to

Auf sie folgt stets der Infinitiv, außer bei Kurzantworten und Fragesätzen:

Can Sally **speak** French well? – Yes, she can, can't she?

Bei Fragen und verneinten Aussagesätzen verwendet man bei Hilfsverben keine Umschreibung mit "do":

Must I help again? – No, thanks, you **needn't help** me now.

Beachte auch die Wortstellung im Relativsatz: Im Gegensatz zum Deutschen behält das Englische **immer**, auch in Nebensätzen, die **Wortstellung S–P–O** (subject – predicate – object) bei.

Gut einprägen solltest du dir auch die Verwendung der Relativpronomen:

***who** benutzt man für **Personen**:*

Is Shakespeare the author who wrote "Hamlet"?

***which** benutzt man für **Dinge**:*

"Hamlet" is a play which is world-famous.

***that** benutzt man für **Personen und Dinge**, d. h. in den obigen Sätzen kannst du sowohl für "who" als auch für "which" das Relativpronomen "that" einsetzen.*

***whose** gilt ebenfalls für **Personen und Dinge** und bedeutet „deren" oder „dessen".*

4.

the name which **has been given** to the huge bell
der Name, den **man** der riesigen Glocke **gegeben hat**
I'm sure you **have seen** pictures of (...) before
sicherlich **haben** Sie schon einmal Bilder von (...) **gesehen**

Die gebrauchte Verbform ist das **present perfect.** Man muss es hier verwenden, um hervorzuheben, dass die Handlung oder ein Zustand der Vergangenheit in einer Beziehung zur Gegenwart steht. Es geht nicht darum, **wann** etwas geschehen ist **(Zeitpunkt)**, sondern **dass** es geschehen ist **(Ergebnis):** Die Abgeschlossenheit der Handlung wird betont. Deshalb steht auch keine feste Zeitangabe wie "last century" (in diesem Fall müsste sonst das simple past verwendet werden!), sondern höchstens ein Zeitadverb, das keinen bestimmten Zeitpunkt ausdrückt, z. B. "before".

Tipp!

Bei Zeitadverbien wie
before – never – just – ever – yet – not yet –
so far – up to now
steht häufig das present perfect!

5.

the Houses of Parliament **stand** on the site
das Parlamentsgebäude **steht** an der Stelle

Die gesuchte Verbform ist das **simple present.** Es drückt hier aus, dass das Parlamentsgebäude immer dort steht. Angenommen, man würde "are standing" sagen, so würde dies heißen, dass das Parlamentsgebäude in London umherzieht und sich zum Zeitpunkt des Sprechens gerade an der Stelle des früheren Königspalastes aufhält. Eine ziemlich absurde Vorstellung!

6.

the Palace **was very badly damaged**
der Palast **wurde sehr schwer beschädigt**

Das Prädikat "was damaged" steht im **simple past passive.** Man verwendet diese Zeit, wenn eine Handlung oder ein Zustand abgeschlossen ist. Nicht selten wird dabei auch der genaue Zeitpunkt genannt, z. B. "in 1834", oder er lässt sich aus dem Textzusammenhang erschließen.

Zeitangaben wie
yesterday – last month – an hour ago – in 1963 –
during the 90s – between March and July
sind Signalwörter für das simple past.

"badly" ist ein Adverb. Im Deutschen lassen sich Adjektiv und Adverb häufig der Form nach nicht unterscheiden. Vergleiche:

*Sandra speaks French **well.*** – *Sandra spricht **gut** Französisch.*
*Sandra's French is **good**.* – *Sandras Französisch ist **gut**.*

Adjektive stehen vor Nomen oder nach einer Form von "be", Adverbien stehen bei Verben auf die Frage „Wie?", „Auf welche Weise geschieht etwas?" und vor Adverbien.

*Sandra rides her bike **dangerously.***
*She rides it **extremely dangerously.***

---

*Im Gegensatz zum Deutschen kann das Adverb der Art und Weise **nie** zwischen Prädikat und direktem Objekt stehen. Vergleiche:*

*He **quickly** adopts new ideas.*
oder: – *Er greift **schnell** neue Ideen auf.*
*He adopts new ideas **quickly**.*

7.

all that **could be saved**
alles, was **gerettet werden konnte**

Die Bildung des **Passivs mit einem Hilfsverb**, hier "could", kennst du bereits. Beachte auch die Wortstellung des zusammengesetzten Prädikats. Sie folgt immer der Wortstellung im Aussagesatz: "Westminster Hall could be saved."

Nach "all", "everything" und "nothing" wird nur "that" verwendet:

***Nothing that** Marc said was really true.* – ***Nichts, was** Marc sagte, war wirklich wahr.*

8.

one of the **finest** halls
eine der **schönsten** Hallen

Die Erläuterung zur Steigerung der Adjektive findest du unter **2**.

9.

since 1066, all English kings and queens **have been crowned** in this church
seit 1066 **werden** alle englischen Könige und Königinnen in dieser Kirche **gekrönt**

Im Deutschen verwenden wir das Präsens, im Englischen muss jedoch das present perfect gesetzt werden. Nach Zeitangaben wie **since, for, all day** benutzt man das **present perfect** bzw., wenn man den Ablauf einer Handlung betonen möchte, das **present perfect progressive.** Im Deutschen steht hier häufig das Präsens mit „schon“.

*Sowohl "since" als auch "for" bedeuten im Deutschen „seit“. Ausdrücke mit **since** bezeichnen einen **Zeitpunkt,** Ausdrücke mit **for** einen **Zeitraum:***

*The Queen has been paying taxes **since the mid-nineties.***
*The Queen has been paying taxes **for several years.***

10.

many famous people **are buried** here
viele berühmte Menschen **sind** hier **begraben**

Die Umwandlung des "-y" in "-ie" geschieht in folgenden Fällen:
- bei der Pluralbildung: city – cit**ies**
- bei der 3. Person Singular simple present:

  Dave always worr**ies** (to worry) about his marks.

- bei der Bildung des simple past bzw. des past participle der regelmäßigen Verben:

  The child cr**ied** (to cry) after her pet had been carr**ied** (to carry) away.
- bei der Bildung des Komparativs bzw. Superlativs:

  This is the funn**iest** (funny) joke I've ever heard.
- beim Anhängen der Silbe "-ly" an Adverbien: easily (easy).
  Allerdings muss dem "-y" ein Konsonant vorausgehen. Vergleiche:

  Sue rarely **buys toys** for her daughter.

11.

Westminster is also the name **used** for a central London borough
Westminster ist auch **der** Name, **der** für einen Stadtbezirk im Zentrum Londons **benutzt wird**

Die Verbform "used" ist das past participle des Verbs "use". Partizipien stehen häufig anstelle von Relativsätzen. Wenn man im Englischen die Partizipialkonstruktion in den Relativsatz zurückführt, wird die passivische Bedeutung von "used" deutlich:

Westminster is also the name **which/that is used** for a central London borough.

Diese Partizipialkonstruktion kann nur dann verwendet werden, wenn das Relativpronomen – hier "which" oder "that" – Subjekt ist!

12.

which **contains** several important buildings
das mehrere Gebäude **umfasst**
several important buildings **including** Buckingham Palace
mehrere bedeutende Gebäude, die den Buckingham-Palast **einschließen** (oder: **einschließlich** des Buckingham-Palastes)

Die Verben "contain" und "include" gehören zur Gruppe der so genannten "state verbs". Das sind Verben, die nur in Ausnahmefällen die progressive form bilden ("including" ist in diesem Fall eine Partizipialkonstruktion).

Weitere Verben dieser Gruppe sind:
know – understand – like – dislike – want – mean – belong to – consist of

13.

if the flag **is flying** on top
wenn die Fahne oben **weht**

Das Prädikat steht im **present progressive** und drückt hier einen Zustand von begrenzter Dauer aus, d. h. die Fahne weht nur dann oben, wenn die Queen sich gerade in ihrem Palast aufhält. Vergleiche:

Do you **learn** French at school?	Kann man auf eurer Schule Französisch lernen?
Are you **learning** French at school?	Lernst du in der Schule (in diesem Schuljahr) Französisch?

14.

it **means** she is at home
das **heißt**, dass sie zu Hause ist

"Mean" bedeutet nicht „meinen" im Sinne von „glauben", sondern im Sinne von „ausdrücken", „bedeuten", „heißen"!

Ich **meine**, wir sollten jetzt gehen.	I **think** we should go now.
Was **meinst** du damit? Was willst du damit **sagen**?	What **do** you **mean** by that?

15.

most tourists **are attracted** by the Changing of the Guard
die meisten Touristen **werden** durch den Wachwechsel **angezogen**

Die Erläuterung zur Bildung des Passivs findest du unter **1.**

16.

a ceremony **held** in the forecourt of the Palace every morning
eine Zeremonie, **die** jeden Vormittag im Vorhof des Palastes **abgehalten wird**

Die Erläuterung zur Partizipialkonstruktion findest du unter **11.**

17.

the new guard, **led** by a band
die neue Wache, **die** von einer Musikkapelle **angeführt wird**

Hier entspricht die Partizipialkonstruktion wieder einem Relativsatz mit passivischer Bedeutung:

the new guard, **which is led** by a band, (...)

Vielleicht ist dir aufgefallen, dass der Relativsatz im Englischen zwischen Kommas steht. Es handelt sich hierbei um einen so genannten nicht notwendigen Relativsatz ("non-defining relative clause").
Nicht notwendige Relativsätze geben ergänzende Informationen zu den Personen oder Dingen, auf die sie sich beziehen: Auch ohne den Relativsatz ist klar, wer oder was gemeint ist. Sie werden deshalb durch **Kommas** vom Hauptsatz abgetrennt.
In nicht notwendigen Relativsätzen muss stets ein Relativpronomen stehen. Das Relativpronomen "that" ist ausgeschlossen! Im **Subjektsfall** verwendet man **who** (für Personen) und **which** (für Dinge und Tiere). Im Objektsfall stehen **who** bzw. im formellen Englisch **whom** und **which.**

Queen Mum, **who/whom (Objektsfall) the British are very fond of,** turned 100 in the summer of 2000.
The celebrations, **which (Subjektsfall) interested everybody in the nation,** lasted for a couple of weeks.

18.

The new guard (...) **arrives** to take over from the old guard
Die neue Wache (...) **trifft ein,** um die alte Wache abzulösen

Das **simple present** ist erforderlich, weil es sich um einen routinemäßigen Vorgang handelt, der im vorausgehenden Satz durch "every morning" als solcher markiert ist.

19.

Do you **know** (...)
Weißt du (...)

Wann verwendet man die Umschreibung mit "do/does/did"?
- Wenn das Verb ein Vollverb (main verb) und kein Hilfsverb (auxiliary) ist.
  Vollverben sind etwa: work, build, do
  Hilfsverben sind z. B.: can, should, will
- Wenn es sich entweder um einen Fragesatz oder um einen verneinten Aussagesatz handelt.
- Wenn die Zeitform das simple present oder das simple past ist.

20.

the crown jewels **are kept**
die Kronjuwelen **werden aufbewahrt**

Die Erläuterung zur Bildung des Passivs findest du unter **1.**

21.

although he **had fought** against the Spanish Armada
obwohl er gegen die spanische Armada **gekämpft hatte**

Sowohl die Hinrichtung Sir Walter Raleighs als auch seine Kämpfe gegen die spanische Armada sind in der Vergangenheit abgeschlossene Handlungen. Die Kämpfe lagen aber zeitlich vor der Hinrichtung. Dies wird grammatikalisch durch das **past perfect**, die Zeitform der **Vorzeitigkeit**, ausgedrückt.

22.

you **can easily see**
kann man **leicht erkennen**

Die Erläuterung zu den Adverbien findest du unter **6.**

23.

where some old docks **have been closed down**
wo einige alte Docks **stillgelegt wurden/worden sind**

Die Erläuterung zur Verwendung des present perfect findest du unter **4.**

24.

some years ago many poor families **had to** leave the area
vor einigen Jahren **mussten** viele arme Familien das Gebiet verlassen

Das Hilfsverb "must" besitzt keine Vergangenheits- bzw. Futurformen. An seine Stelle tritt die **Ersatzform** "to have to", das jedoch kein Hilfsverb, sondern ein Vollverb ist. Weitere Ersatzformen: "to be able to" für "can", "to be allowed to" für "may".

As a little boy, **did you have to tidy up** your room every week?
– Yes, and my children **will have to do** that as well.
I've never **been able to understand** why your sister did such a silly thing. – Well, our parents **had never allowed** her to go out with friends. So she ran away with Jack.

25.

they could no longer **afford to live** in this rich neighbourhood
sie konnten es sich nicht länger **leisten,** in diesem reichen Viertel **zu wohnen**

Nach "afford" steht der Infinitiv mit "to". Da der Infinitiv mit "to" nach vielen Vollverben steht, ist es ratsam, sich bei jedem neu zu lernenden Verb den Anschluss zu merken, z. B.

to advise somebody to do something	jemandem raten, etwas zu tun

Der Infinitiv **ohne** "to" steht:
- nach den meisten **Hilfsverben:**
  My dad **cannot** roller skate.
- nach Verben, die **Veranlassen oder Zulassen** ausdrücken:
  My dad wants to **make** me show him how to roller skate, but I don't **let** him use my skates.
- nach Verben des **Wahrnehmens und Beobachtens:**
  But yesterday I **saw** him buy a pair in a shop.

26.

although they **would have enjoyed staying** there
obwohl sie **sehr gerne** dort **geblieben wären**

Nach "enjoy" folgt das **Gerundium.** Es steht:
- nach bestimmten Verben:
  Avoid talking to Bill about that topic. It really upsets him.

– nach Verben + Präposition:
OK, I will. I'm really looking forward to meeting him again.
– nach Adjektiv + Präposition:
Me, too. I wonder if he is still good at making cakes.
– nach Nomen + Präposition:
I'm sure he is. I hope we won't have any difficulty in finding his new flat.

27.

at the moment more and more flats **are being built**
zur Zeit **werden** immer mehr Wohnungen **gebaut**

Die gesuchte Verbform heißt **present progressive passive** und wird aufgrund des Signalwortes "at the moment" verwendet. Es setzt sich aus drei Komponenten zusammen: Form von "be" + "being" + past participle.

28.

if the former inhabitants **come** back in a couple of years
wenn/falls die früheren Bewohner in ein paar Jahren **zurückkommen (werden)**

Auch wenn sich in einem if-Satz die erfüllbare Bedingung („zurückkommen werden") auf die Zukunft ("in a couple of years") bezieht, darf man dort nie das will-future benutzen. Es muss das **simple present** stehen.

29.

they **won't recognize** their area any longer
sie **werden** ihr Wohngebiet nicht mehr **wiedererkennen**

Hier dagegen drückt der Hauptsatz die Folge für die Zukunft aus, daher steht das **will-future.**

30.

it **will have completely changed**
es **wird sich völlig verändert haben**

Die benötigte Zeitform ist das **future perfect.** Es wird gebildet aus "will" + "have" + past participle und drückt aus, dass eine Handlung zu einem bestimmten Zeitpunkt in der Zukunft abgeschlossen sein wird.

31.

an elderly lady recently said she **didn't want** to go back
to the place because it **was** too sad for her
eine ältere Frau sagte neulich, dass sie dorthin
nicht mehr zurückkehren **wolle**, weil es zu traurig für sie **sei**

Das Prädikat "said" im Hauptsatz leitet hier die **indirekte Rede** (indirect speech) ein. Einige Verben, die die indirekte Rede einleiten können (introductory verbs):

add – advise – agree – answer – ask – be sorry – be sure – complain – explain – feel – hope – know – promise – remember – reply – say – suggest – tell (someone) – think – want to know – wonder

Steht das einleitende Verb im simple past (nicht im simple present!), werden die Zeiten nach bestimmten Regeln verschoben. Diese Zeitenverschiebung bezeichnet man als backshift of tenses. Sie gilt sowohl für die simple form als auch für die progressive form.

direct speech	→	*indirect speech*
1. simple present and auxiliary verbs	→	*simple past*
2. present perfect	→	*past perfect*
3. simple past	→	*past perfect*
4. past perfect	→	*past perfect*
5. will-future	→	*conditional ("would")*

direct speech	**indirect speech**
1. "I **love** dancing, but I **can't** break-dance."	He said (that) he **loved** dancing but he **couldn't** break-dance.
2. "I**'ve been dancing** for five years."	He told me (that) he **had been dancing** for five years.
3. "Once I **broke** my leg in a competition."	He added (that) once he **had broken** his leg in a competition.
4. "**Had** it ever **happened** to you before?"	I asked him if it **had** ever **happened** to him before.
5. "No and I wish it **will** never **happen** again."	He said no and wished it **would** never **happen** again.

Tipp!

Um die korrekte Zeitform des Prädikats in der indirekten Rede herauszufinden, ist es sinnvoll, den Satz zunächst in die direkte Rede zurückzuverwandeln:

indirekte Rede:

Mein Freund fragte mich, wie viele Preise ich schon gewonnen habe.

direkte Rede:

„Wie viele Preise hast du schon gewonnen?

"How many prizes ***have*** *you already* ***won?"*** *(present perfect)*

indirekte Rede:

My friend asked me how many prizes I ***had*** *already* ***won.*** *(past perfect)*

Zusammenfassen von Texten – Summary Writing

Das Schreiben von Zusammenfassungen (summaries) erfordert ein wenig Übung und Ausdauer, da man bei den ersten Versuchen dazu neigt, zu lange Texte zu verfassen und das Original nachzuerzählen.

Zu welchem Zweck schreibt man summaries?
Mit einem summary sollst du unter Beweis stellen, dass du

1. das Hauptthema eines Textes erfassen und
2. die wesentlichen Punkte danach inhaltlich und sprachlich gestrafft wiedergeben kannst.

Was ist beim Verfassen von summaries zu beachten?
Englischsprachige Zusammenfassungen

- sollten im Idealfall nur ein Drittel so lang sein wie das Original. Diese vorgeschriebene Länge kann bis zu 10 % überschritten werden (lästiges Wörterzählen wird sich daher leider nicht vermeiden lassen).
- geben dir die Möglichkeit, mit deinen eigenen sprachlichen Mitteln auszudrücken, worum es im Originaltext geht. Dabei darf man sich vom Stil und Wortschatz des Originals lösen: Man sollte z. B. nicht versuchen, den englischen Satzbau oder Stil des vorgelegten Textes zu imitieren. Die Übernahme von Formulierungen aus dem Text wird als "copying" (Abschreiben) angesehen und ist selbstverständlich tabu.
- geben nur das Wesentliche, das Herz einer Passage wieder. Daher sind Beispiele, Vergleiche, Wiederholungen und überflüssige Details sowie direkte Rede nicht erlaubt. Werden im Originaltext Gedanken an mehreren Stellen ausgedrückt, musst du bei einer Zusammenfassung entscheiden, an welcher Stelle der Punkt am sinnvollsten erwähnt wird.

- werden aus der Sicht des Autors geschrieben, dessen Werk man zusammenfasst. Daher kann man sich "The author says ..." oder "The paragraph is about ..." o. ä. sparen. Am besten tut man so, als fasse man seinen eigenen Text zusammen – natürlich ohne eigene Stellungnahme!

Wie schreibt man erfolgreich summaries?
Am besten befolgst du die folgenden sechs Arbeitsschritte:

1. Lies den zusammenzufassenden Text ganz genau durch.

2. Beantworte dir die Frage „Was will der Autor mit diesem Text sagen?“ in einem Satz, um eine klare Vorstellung vom Thema zu haben. Schreibe diese Antwort auf.

3. Da du deinen eigenen Wortschatz unter Beweis stellen sollst, erinnere dich an die wichtigsten Schlüsselwörter (keywords), Verben und feststehenden Ausdrücke aus dem Wortfeld, das zum betreffenden Thema gehört. Notiere diese spontanen Einfälle.
   Sollte der Originaltext Fachausdrücke (technical terms) enthalten, dürfen diese zur Not beibehalten werden. Besser ist es jedoch, wenn man gleichbedeutende Umschreibungen (synonymous expressions) findet und/oder mehrere Fachausdrücke unter einem Oberbegriff zusammenfasst.

4. Suche die Hauptinhaltspunkte und ordne sie auf deinem Konzeptblatt in sinnvoller Reihenfolge an.

5. Schreibe eine Rohfassung deines summary. Verknüpfe dabei möglichst deine Ideen durch so genannte "linkers", wie die Übersetzungen für „(je)doch“ – "but", "yet" (am Satzanfang mit Komma), "however" (Stellung zumeist zwischen Kommata nach dem Subjekt) oder Entsprechungen von „daher“, „folglich“ – "so", "therefore", "consequently".
   Abrupte Satzübergänge können durch Ausdrücke wie "moreover", "besides" – „darüber hinaus“ oder "on the other hand" (nicht "side"!) – „andererseits“ vermieden werden.
   Stilistisch empfehlenswert ist es auch, einige Ideen anderen unterzuordnen und Nebensätze mit Konjunktionen wie "although" –

„obwohl“, “since” oder “as” – „da“, „weil“ oder “in order to” + Infinitiv – „um zu“ beginnen zu lassen.

6. Lies dein summary **kritisch** nach:

   - Überprüfe, ob du die erlaubte Höchstzahl an Wörtern nicht überschritten hast. Dabei empfiehlt es sich, die Wörter paarweise zu zählen und nach jeweils 50 Wörtern eine Bleistiftmarkierung anzubringen, damit man, falls man sich verzählen sollte, nicht noch einmal von Anfang an nachzählen muss.
   - Überprüfe, ob du am Stil des Geschriebenen noch etwas verbessern kannst (durch Einfügen von “linkers”, durch treffendere Ausdrücke oder durch Veränderung des Satzbaus usw.), um keine Monotonie aufkommen zu lassen.

Übrigens: Deine Antworten werden wahrscheinlich nicht identisch mit denen im Lösungsteil sein. Wir haben versucht, dir Musterantworten zu geben – es ist jedoch kein Beinbruch, wenn deine Lösungen einfacher formuliert sind.

2.1 Canada's Native People

Canada's Indians and Inuit are proud to be called the country's native population. They have influenced Canadian life in many ways and remain a culturally active force.

The Indians have struggled for generations against assimilation into the non-native milieu. In the past 40 years, the Inuit and Indian lifestyles in northern Canada have undergone great changes with the intrusion of technology and culture from southern Canada. Inevitably, new social problems have followed.

Encouraged by the government, Canada's native peoples are seeking to adopt the practical elements of modern society that best suit their needs while maintaining many aspects of their traditional ways of life.

In recent years, there has been renewed interest in both Indian and Inuit arts, which have gained international acclaim. As a result, aboriginal rights – the property rights claimed by them – have become an important issue.

(139 Wörter)

2.2 Television Programmes

If you keep a record of your television viewing for a few days, you will be surprised to see how long this activity takes. Have you learned to evaluate the programmes you see during these hours?

There are various kinds of television programmes. Some are intended to provide information and to stimulate thinking. These include talks, travel films, discussions and the news.

A second kind of television programme is intended purely for entertainment. This kind includes comedies, westerns, detective stories and programmes that feature popular music and dancing.

There is nothing wrong with entertainment as long as it entertains. Most people enjoy it. Everyone has the right to decide what he or she enjoys. It is up to you to determine what you enjoy and how you want to spend your time. Are you really entertained by all the programmes you see?

(140 Wörter)

2.3 Modern Magic

In his fantasy "A Midsummer Night's Dream", Shakespeare lets Puck say that he will circle the earth in forty minutes. But as great as his imagination was, Shakespeare never conceived that one day man would be able to circle the earth with words and images in a fraction of a second.

Today, through the media of radio and television, communication has become almost instantaneous – even over great distances. Television and radio are truly modern magic. With the coming of the age of science, technical achievements have been multiplied beyond earlier man's wildest dreams.

Not even Aladdin and his miracle-working lamp had as much magic as the millions of families who have access to television and radio. By pressing a button, one can bring music, sports, and world events into the living room. You have instant contact with virtually the entire world. Do you always use this magic lamp wisely?

(149 Wörter)

Leseverständnis – Reading Comprehension

Tipps zur Arbeitstechnik

1. Lies den jeweiligen Text sorgfältig durch und versuche, dir einen Überblick über den gesamten Text zu verschaffen.
2. Wenn du ein Wort nicht verstehst, versuche, den Sinn aus dem Satz- oder Textzusammenhang zu erschließen – beachte jedoch, dass du dich nicht zu lange damit aufhältst.
3. Wenn du den Text gelesen hast, versuche, dich an möglichst viele Inhaltspunkte zu erinnern, ohne auf den Text zu schauen.
4. Lies die Fragen langsam durch. Beachte besonders: Voraussetzung für die richtige Beantwortung der Frage ist, dass du die Frage richtig erfasst hast. Ohne Frageverständnis keine richtigen Antworten!
5. Präge dir die erste Frage ein und suche die Stelle im Text, die dir die Antwort ermöglicht. Unterstreiche diese Stelle. Beantworte in dieser Weise die nachfolgenden Fragen.

Read the text – answer the questions – do the exercises!

3.1 The Big Apple

When you approach New York from the sea you are overwhelmed by the sight of the famous skyline. You pass the Statue of Liberty which rises about 300 feet from a small island in the middle of the harbour. The statue was given by the people of France to the people of the US in 1884, in memory of the French and the American Revolution.
New York was founded by Dutch merchants and immigrants at the beginning of the 17th century, and was originally called New Amsterdam. The oldest and most important part of the city is the island of Manhattan. Here you can see the Manhattan skyline whose towering buildings of steel and glass have attracted people from all over the world. Generations of immigrants have come with their hopes and fears to Manhattan.
New York, a cosmopolitan city of about eight million inhabitants, is a melting pot of people of all nationalities. There are, for example more Germans in New York than in Cologne, more Italians than in Palermo, more Jews than in the whole of Israel. Even today, there is a constant flow of new arrivals. The majority of these come from

Middle America and Southern Europe. Tremendous problems arise from the task of assimilating the immigrants from different origins and races.

New York is a city of immense vitality and great energy which seem to radiate from her streets and avenues. Here is Times Square, the famous crossing of Broadway and 7th Avenue. Its huge billboard advertisements flash on and off 24 hours a day. Times Square is the centre of New York's theatre district.
New York is also a city of contrasts. East Harlem, at a small distance from Broadway, is one of the worst slum districts in the world. More than 200,000 coloured people live here in unsanitary buildings, without sufficient water, heating or electricity in a world of poverty and crime.

Words from the text you may not know:

to approach	sich nähern
to arise	entstehen
to assimilate	aufnehmen
avenue	Prachtstraße

billboard advertisement	Reklametafel
cosmopolitan	international
crossing	Kreuzung
to flash	blitzen, funkeln
flow	Strom, Fluss
to found	gründen
harbour	Hafen
melting pot	Schmelztiegel
merchant	Kaufmann, Händler
in memory of	zur Erinnerung an
original	ursprünglich
to overwhelm	überwältigen
poverty	Armut
to radiate	ausstrahlen
to rise	sich erheben
steel	Stahl
sufficient	genügend, ausreichend
task	Aufgabe
to tower	aufragen
tremendous	riesig
unsanitary	unhygienisch

Fragen zum Text

A 1 Answer in complete sentences.

1. Which historical events does the Statue of Liberty recall?
2. Why did New York originally have a Dutch name?
3. Why do you think there are so many immigrants from foreign countries? What do they hope to find?
4. For which reasons did people emigrate to America in the past centuries?
5. Describe the contrasts which you find in New York (two items).
6. What is a slum district like according to the text?

Wortschatz

A 2 Find the sentence with a similar meaning and mark it off with a cross.

1. New York is a melting pot of people of all nationalities.
   ( ) In New York, you can meet a lot of people from all over the world.
   ( ) In New York, people of different nations are transformed into Americans.
   ( ) New York accepts people from all over the world.
   ( ) In New York, people of all nationalities live together.

2. You are overwhelmed by the sight of the skyline.
   ( ) You feel uneasy when you see the vast horizon.
   ( ) You wonder at the sight of the line in the sky.
   ( ) You are confused when you see the outline of the skyscrapers against the sky.
   ( ) You are very astonished when you see the sky-high buildings.

A 3 Find a synonym (or a synonymous expression) for the bold (fett gedruckt) expressions. Write the complete sentences in your notebook!

1. We **approached** the harbour.
2. We came **in sight of** the statue.
3. The Dutch **founded** a colony.
4. The Dutch were the **original** founders.
5. There is a **constant** flow of people.
6. The **majority of** these people are poor.
7. It's a **tremendous** problem.
8. They live **without sufficient** water.
9. It's **a small distance** off Broadway.

A 4 Explain the following bold expressions in one sentence.

1. A **famous** sight: a sight which is ______________________.
2. A **cosmopolitan** city: a city in which ____________________

   ______________________________.
3. A **towering** building: a building which ___________________.

A 5 Fill in the missing words!

verb	noun	adjective
to radiate		
to attract	attraction	attractive
	fear	
	vitality	
–	energy	
	advertisement	
	original	original
–	import	important
	difference	different

A 6 Word building: A number of words can take the ending "-ful" and/or "-less". Example: hope – hopeful – hopeless. Which of the following words can take **1.** both endings, **2.** only "-less", **3.** only "-ful"?

fear – harm – thank – use – success
need – forget – care – rest – help

Grammatik

A 7 Articles: Which of the following expressions take the definite article? Make two lists: **list 1** with the definite article, **list 2** without definite article.

_______ Statue of Liberty, _______ Manhattan Island, _______ Empire State Building, _______ United States of America, _______ North America, _______ Israel, _______ Southern Europe, _______ President Nixon, _______ President of _______ US, _______ Times Square, _______ Broadway, by _______ night, during _______ night, at _______ night, throughout _______ night, _______ capitalism, to go by _______ sea, in _______ sea, in _______ memory of, at _______ first sight, in _______ public, with _______ help of, on _______ condition that

A 8 Fill in the definite article where necessary.

1. For people in slums _______ winter is a hard season.
2. I remember _______ winter of the year 1973.
3. Many immigrants expected to find _______ gold.
4. During the gold rush, a lot of them moved on westward to find _______ gold of which they had heard.
5. The immigrants knew that _______ life would be hard.
6. But they were not afraid of _______ life which expected them.
7. The highest building in every settlement was _______ church.
8. Every Sunday they went to _______ church.
9. On Thanksgiving Day they invited their friends for __________ dinner.

10. They enjoyed ______ dinner which consisted of roast turkey and plum pudding.
11. They made ______ peace with the Indians.
12. When more and more immigrants came, ______ peace made by the first settlers was broken.

A 9 Form sentences from the following words.

1. twice/they/paid/price/the
2. were/both/boys/the/late
3. I/in/did/the/time/half/it
4. double/he/the/amount/asked/for
5. all/people/shouting/the/were
6. people/the/drive/faster/more/will/the/occur/accidents

A 10 Which of the following expressions take the indefinite article? Make two lists: **list 1** with the indefinite article, **list 2** without the indefinite article.

I'm in ______ hurry, she has ______ headache, they made ______ way for the king, he is ______ Frenchman, he took ______ seat, there is ______ lot of time, there is ______ plenty of time, there is ______ good news, as ______ rule, she took ______ notice of him, he will arrive in ______ time.

A 11 Complete the sentences in the plural and add "some" if necessary.

1. My brother is an artist. – My brothers are ____________________.
2. Here's a bottle of wine. – Here are ____________________ of wine.
3. John is an American. – John and Mary are ____________________.
4. Peter has a nice book. – Peter has ____________________.
5. Tom became an engineer. – Tom and Bob became ____________________.
6. He is known as a good player. – They are known as ____________________.
7. He had a sandwich for lunch. – I had ____________________ for lunch.
8. I heard a voice. – I heard ____________________.
9. What a pretty girl! – What ____________________!

A 12 Fill in: "a" or "one".

1. ________ rainy day is very common in England, when we were there, we had ________ day of sunshine.
2. ________ bar of chocolate ________ day doesn't do any harm.
3. ________ knife is no good for little children. ________ knife is no good for a cook, he needs several.
4. Do you need ________ sheet of paper? – Yes, thank you, ________ sheet will be enough.
5. Tom is ________ friend of mine. Tom is ________ of my friends.

A 13 Form correct sentences:

1. I/such/have/a/never/building/before/seen
2. bought/a/pound/I/half
3. it/a/6p/costs/dozen
4. never/a/sailor/many/returned
5. quite/this/a/is/thing/good

A 14 Prepositions and adverbial particles: Complete the following sentences by using an expression with "at".

1. I don't know what to do. – I'm ____________________ what to do.
2. Sometimes I think he is mad. – ________________________ I think he is mad.
3. Don't interrupt me while I'm working . – Don't interrupt me while I'm ______________________.
4. The Indians fought against the Whites. – The Indians were __________________________ with the Whites.
5. She liked him from the moment she saw him. – She liked him _______________________.
6. Finally she came. – ______________________ she came.
7. He came immediately. – He came ______________________.
8. Now I can't help you. – ______________________ I can't help you.

Rechtschreibung

A 15 Find a homophone for the following words taken from the text.

sea – _____________ , steel – _____________ , whole – _____________ ,
new – ______________ , hour – ______________

A 16 Rewrite these words, adding a second consonant where necessary.

a ____ proach, a ____ pologize, i ____ migrant, e ____ migrant,

a ____ similate, a ____ bundant, a ____ dress, di ____ sappear,

i ____ magine, i ____ mitate, i ____ mense, i ____ mediately,

i ____ numerable, po ____ sess, o ____ pinion

3.2 The American Frontier

In normal use the word frontier denotes that part of a country which borders on another country. Speaking of America, the term "frontier" has quite a different meaning. It comprises the region where the first settlers fought against the wilderness, the forces of nature, and the Indians.

When their settlements became too small because of the growing number of newcomers, people had to push this frontier westward to find new land. This westward-moving expansion came to a halt in 1890, when the pioneers had reached the Pacific Ocean.

The pioneers had to be strong and fearless to be able to live in a hostile environment. Every day they were faced with new dangers.

The immigrants had hardly arrived on the frontier when they were confronted with immense problems. They were deprived of a lot of things which they had taken for granted in Europe. They were forced

to acquire new skills, which ranged from hunting to farming, and from log house building to shoe mending.
Money or a title counted for little, what was essential was their inventiveness, and their ability to overcome the difficulties. Rarely was there help from the government, it took days to travel to a doctor, seldom could the pioneers expect to be protected by soldiers. Life on the frontier was extremely hard.
We find certain features in the American character, which may have been produced by frontier life. The American people are known to be practical-minded. The proverb "necessity is the mother of invention" explains this attitude. At the same time they are said to achieve their aims with restless energy.
The Americans' self-reliance has often been criticised. To Europeans their optimism often seems exaggerated. But there is no denying the fact that the American people have, in less than four centuries, transformed a wilderness into one of the most powerful countries of the world.

Words from the text you may not know:

ability	Fähigkeit
to achieve	leisten, erreichen
to acquire	erwerben
aim	Ziel
attitude	Haltung, Einstellung
to border on	angrenzen
to count for little	wenig wert sein
to denote	bezeichnen
to deny	widerlegen, abstreiten
to deprive	entziehen, vorenthalten
essential	wesentlich
to expect	erwarten
exaggerated	übertrieben
expansion	Ausdehnung, -breitung
to face	gegenüberstehen
feature	Merkmal
frontier	(Zivilisations-)Grenze

hostile	feindlich
invention	Erfindung
inventiveness	Erfindungsgabe
log house	Blockhaus
necessity	Notwendigkeit
to overcome	bezwingen
practical-minded	praktisch orientiert
proverb	Sprichwort
to range	reichen
from ... to	von ... bis
self-reliance	Selbstsicherheit, -ständigkeit
shoe mending	Schuhe flicken
skills	Fähigkeiten
to take for granted	für selbstverständlich erachten

Fragen zum Text

A 1 Answer in complete sentences.

1. What does "frontier" mean in this context?
2. Describe the dangers the pioneers were faced with (three items).
3. Explain in your own words: "Necessity is the mother of invention."
4. Give reasons for the statement: America is one of the most powerful countries in the world (three items).

Wortschatz

A 2 Find the sentence with a similar meaning and mark it off with a cross.

1. They were forced to acquire new skills.
   ( ) They had to make new efforts.
   ( ) They were compelled to gain new abilities for themselves.
   ( ) They were obliged to assimilate themselves in the New World.
   ( ) It was necessary for them to obtain a new job.

2. To Europeans, their optimism often seems exaggerated.
   ( ) To Europeans, their confidence often seems ridiculous.
   ( ) Europeans often think that their belief in success is too optimistic.
   ( ) To Europeans, their outlook on life often seems naive.
   ( ) Europeans often find that they are over-optimistic.

A 3 Find the opposites of the following adjectives taken from the text.

1. different ______________
2. growing ______________
3. strong ______________
4. hostile ______________
5. the best ______________

A 4 Find the verbs which correspond to the following nouns.

1. meaning ______________
2. expansion ______________
3. inventiveness ______________
4. product ______________
5. solution ______________
6. reliance ______________

A 5 Find a synonym for the expressions. Write in your notebook.

1. in normal use
2. it denotes
3. they became too small
4. a growing number of
5. they had reached
6. fearless
7. they were faced with
8. they were deprived of
9. to overcome difficulties
10. restless energy

A 6 Word building: Find the nouns corresponding to the following words.

1. to speak ____________
2. wild ____________
3. to grow ____________
4. strong ____________
5. hostile ____________
6. to survive ____________
7. essential ____________
8. necessary ____________

A 7 To which of the following words can you add "self-"? Write them in your notebook.

reliance – courage – service – control – protection
respect – work – interest – made – cooked

A 8 Combine the words with each word in the list that follows.

1. work: home, book
2. house: log, wife, country, hold
3. day: birth, break, pay, time
4. paper: bag, news, money, writing
5. master: head, piece, school, stroke

A 9 Which of the following words ending in "-ing" can you put into the plural? Add "-s" where possible!

building __ , hunting __ , meaning __ , farming __ , painting __ ,

working __ , smoking __ , drawing __

Grammatik

A 10 Word order: Rewrite the following sentences beginning with the negative adverbial in brackets.

example:

The pioneers were helped by the government (seldom).
Seldom were the pioneers helped by the government.

1. The Indians had attacked the camp (in vain).
2. There has been a peaceful time (seldom).
3. Their settlements had become too small, the settlers moved westward (no sooner – than).
4. They had arrived, and they had to fight (hardly – than).
5. There was peace (at no time).

A 11 Rewrite the following sentences, replacing the bold nouns by pronouns.

example:

He sold **the settlers medicine.**
He sold it to them.

1. They sent **the Indians a present.**
2. He gave **the Indian a gun.**
3. He bought **his wife a present.**
4. I described **the situation to my friend.**
5. He took off **his hat.**
6. She put on **her coat.**
7. He laid down **his rifle.**

A 12 Rewrite the following sentences, beginning them with the given expression.

1. Where are the settlers going to? – He wants to know ...
2. Where must I go? – Can you tell me ...
3. Where is the gold hidden? – Show me ...
4. Why are they leaving the settlement? – Tell me why ...

A 13 Rewrite the following sentences, adding first the expression a), then the expression b). The objects should be arranged in their normal order.

1. The settler lent his axe – a) his neighbour, b) his neighbour who lived 20 miles away.
2. He showed the gold – a) his friends, b) all his curious friends and neighbours.
3. He explained his plan – a) me, b) everyone who wanted to know it.

A 14 Prepositions and adverbial particles: Find a synonymous expression for the complete sentence with "from".

1. The train leaves New York at nine. – The train ____________________ from New York at nine.
2. Who sent that letter? – __________________________that letter from?
3. Don't go near the tracks! – ________________________ from the tracks!
4. They worked all day long. – They worked from ___________________ ________________________.
5. They travelled to different places. – They travelled from ____.
6. The two boys are different. – The two boys ________________________ from ________________________.

A 15 Complete the following imperatives.

1. The soup is excellent, eat it ___________!
2. You are not allowed in here, get ___________!
3. Don't touch the painting, hands ___________!
4. Look ___________! There's a car coming.
5. Don't stop working, carry ___________!
6. Don't chew chewing gum in class, ___________ with it!

3.3 Wales and the Welsh

There is hardly any other part of the British Isles where the national spirit is stronger and where national traditions are more cherished pflegen than in Wales. Although it is now about seven hundred years since England and Wales became part of the same kingdom, the Welsh have succeeded in retaining their own individuality and language – up to this day. beibehalten

The Welsh, who are very musical people, are fond of singing songs, of dancing old folk dances and of reciting poetry. There is an annual contest, the Eisteddfod [aɪ'steðvəd], where people have the chance of expressing themselves in verse, in music and in dancing. These meetings sometimes last for a week.

Wales contains some of the finest scenery in Britain. Apart from the mountains it offers limitless tracts of wild and remote country. North

beinhalten

Wales with Snowdonia is a tourist's paradise, and campers will find a large number of convenient sites in glorious surroundings. Wales possesses a magnificent coastline with numerous seaside resorts, delightful shores and bays.
Although nearly all Welsh people can speak English, many speak English and Welsh equally well. Welsh is very similar to Breton, and Bretons can make themselves understood fairly easily in South Wales. The Welsh have a large collection of books printed in Welsh and manuscripts in their National Library at Aberystwyth [æbəˈrɪstwɪθ]. There are also Welsh newspapers and a Welsh radio station with programmes in Welsh on radio and TV.
An Englishman's remark about the Welsh could be: "The Welshman? An untrustworthy fellow, possibly the worst of the lot. He is even meaner than the Scot. He has a queer accent, which we have never been able to get used to, and, when he speaks his impossible language, he always seems to be making fun of us."
What would the Welshman reply: "The Englishman? Oh yes, we were talking about him – not a bad chap, really, but it would be quite easy to do without him. Then again, he has absolutely no sense of music at all."

Words from the text you may not know:

annual	jährlich
Breton	Bretone, bretonisch
to cherish	hegen, pflegen
chap	Bursche
to contain	beinhalten
contest	Wettstreit
to do without sth./sb.	ohne etw./jmd. auskommen
fellow	Bursche
lot	Gruppe, Haufen
mean (BE)	geizig
to recite	rezitieren
remark	Bemerkung, Äußerung
to retain	beibehalten
scenery	Landschaft
untrustworthy	unzuverlässig

Fragen zum Text

A 1 Answer in complete sentences.

1. Name two facts that make Wales different from any other part of the British Isles.
2. Have England and Wales always been part of the same kingdom?
3. What have the Welsh a great liking for?
4. What are campers attracted by in North Wales?
5. Why do many tourists go to the seaside?
6. Why can people from South Wales and people from northern France understand each other?
7. Whose remarks are more polite – the Englishman's or the Welshman's?

Wortschatz

A 2 Explain in your own words. Write in your notebook.

1. annual contest
2. remote country
3. glorious surroundings
4. Welsh is similar to Breton.

A 3 Choose the right word!

1. strength, power, force

   This is a horse of great ____________________.

   The President of the USA has great ____________________.

   He was arrested by means of ____________________.

2. shore, coast, banks, beach

   Aberystwyth lies on the ____________________ of Wales.

   We walked along the ____________________ of the Irish Sea.

   We lay in the sun on a sandy ____________________.

   The river overflowed its ____________________.

3. country, land, nation, county, soil, ground

   Wales is a beautiful ____________________.

   Yorkshire is a ____________________ of England.

   The king gave some ____________________ / ____________________ to his children.

   Next time I shall travel by ____________________

   The ____________________ of this country is exhausted.

   The President's speech deserves ____________________-wide attention.

Grammatik

A 4 Verbs followed by a gerund, an infinitive, or both. Read through this list of words and add the correct preposition if necessary.

to succeed ________ , to apologize ________ , to appreciate ________ , to continue ________ , to hope ________ , to mind ________ , to insist ________ , to rely ________ , to enjoy ________ , to manage ________ , to object ________ , to refuse ________ , to want ________ , to like ________

A 5 Which verbs in the above list are followed by 1. a gerund?, 2. an infinitive?, 3. a gerund or an infinitive? Write in your notebook!

A 6 Fill in gerund or infinitive.

1. They want (speak) ______________________ their own language.
2. They appreciate (speak) __________________ foreign languages.
3. They are fond (do) ___________________ these things.
4. They aim (understand) _______________________ foreigners.
5. They are accustomed (speak) _______________________ English.
6. They are keen (have) _______________________ their own radio station.
7. You can rely (hear) _____________________ the Welsh language.
8. He hesitated (visit) _______________________ Aberystwyth.
9. Bob thought (go) _______________________ to Wales.
10. The Welsh are proud (be) ___________________ musical people.

11. The English never stop (make) ________________________ jokes about the Welsh.

12. Many English would like (understand) ________________________ the Welsh language.

13. Did you manage (see) ________________________ the film about climbing in Wales?

14. I regret not (see) ________________________ the glorious seaside.

15. How about (go) ________________________ to Wales next year?

A 7 Replace the following if-clauses using the -ing-form.

1. You will enjoy your holidays if you go to Wales.
2. If you learn Welsh, you will be able to understand a Breton.
3. You might understand something if you listened attentively.

A 8 Link the sentences using a gerund.

1. Welsh children learn Welsh. They have the chance.
2. They learn this subject at school. Why do they get the opportunity?
3. The English do not speak Welsh. They have no reason for it.
4. The Welsh have their own TV programme. They insist on it.
5. John is Welsh. He is proud of it.
6. The teacher blames Bob. Bob did not do his homework.
7. People stand in queues. They don't care for it.
8. You should listen to me. Don't waste your time.
9. They entered the room. They didn't knock on the door.
10. He escaped from prison. He jumped over the fence.

A 9 Fill in the correct preposition after verbs.

1. Sheila is looking forward __________ speaking Welsh.
2. She speaks __________ learning Breton as well.
3. She dreams __________ understanding all dialects.
4. She aims __________ teaching her brother this language.
5. She objects __________ being disturbed all the time.

A 10 Fill in the correct preposition after adjectives.

1. The English are good __________ making fun of the Welsh.
2. The Welsh are fond __________ singing folk songs.
3. Not all Welsh people are accustomed ____________ speaking English.
4. Are you capable __________ learning Welsh?
5. I am fond __________ listening to Welsh songs.

A 11 Fill in the correct preposition after nouns.

1. John has much pleasure __________ reading books.
2. Many English people have difficulty __________ understanding Welsh.
3. I'll get the opportunity __________ touring through Britain.
4. He takes a delight __________ travelling.
5. What are his reasons __________ leaving the country?

3.4 Indian Traditions in the West

This summer a 26-year-old Indian schoolteacher who has been in Britain for eight years will marry a man she hardly knows – because of her love for her parents who have arranged the marriage.

The girl said: "I wanted to fall in love like Western girls, marry the man of my choice and live a happy, normal life. But I don't want to do anything to hurt my parents, and if I chose a husband for myself, they would think it brought shame on the family."

Ranjana, educated at an Indian boarding school before coming to England, persuaded her parents to agree to one thing – a 60-minute meeting with her husband-to-be. He is a physics teacher.

She teaches at a girls' secondary modern school. She explained her personal dilemma. The Eastern tradition is that parents arrange their children's marriages, but she prefers the Western tradition and feels that a girl should have the right to marry the man she loves.

"I am completely against arranged marriages", said Ranjana. "The idea of meeting your husband-to-be for the first time on the day of your wedding is horrible. I have argued for a long time with my parents over the question of marriage. I am used to being away from home and at 26, I feel I should be allowed to make my own decisions. I kept thinking that maybe I would meet someone and fall in love and be able to persuade my parents that this is the better way."

"But the tradition is so strong that it prevents you from falling in love, because you know nothing can come of it. In a way I can see the value of the Indian tradition. It keeps the family together in a way you don't have now in the West. But for a woman who is used to independence there can be nothing worse than to realize that your marriage will put a complete end to all your freedom."

"So I insisted upon seeing this man my parents had chosen for me – for one hour", Ranjana said. "I travelled to Nottingham to see him at his parents' home. He has lived in England most of his 27 years. When we met we were both rather embarrassed. Both his parents and mine were there at first, and then they left us alone. It was a very strange situation to be in. There were so many things I wanted to ask him, but I simply couldn't . After all, he was a complete stranger."

"I still can't believe that the next time I meet him will be on our wedding day. We shall marry in a Sikh temple in Leamington. It will not be a magnificent affair. I am certain of one thing. If I have children, they will be free to choose their own partners."

Words from the text you may not know:

to argue	sich streiten
choice	Wahl
decision	Entscheidung
embarrassed	verlegen, peinlich berührt
to hurt	verletzen
husband-to-be	zukünftiger Ehemann
to insist on/upon	bestehen auf
magnificent	großartig
to persuade	überreden
to prevent from	hindern an
shame	Schande
to be used to	gewöhnt sein an
value	Wert
wedding	Hochzeit

Fragen zum Text

A 1 Answer in complete sentences.

1. How old was Ranjana when she came to Britain?
2. Why will Ranjana marry a man she hardly knows?
3. Explain Ranjana's attitude toward marriage.
4. What is Ranjana afraid of if she
   a) agrees to the arranged marriage?
   b) refuses to the arranged marriage?
5. Which value does Ranjana see in an arranged marriage?
6. Explain Ranjana's statement: "It will not be a magnificent affair."
7. Will Ranjana keep the Indian tradition of arranged marriages?

Wortschatz

A 2 Find the sentence with a similar meaning and mark it off with a cross.

1. Ranjana persuaded her parents to agree to the meeting.
   ( ) Ranjana continued to ask her parents for an agreement on the meeting.
   ( ) Ranjana convinced her parents to consent to the meeting.
   ( ) Ranjana's parents agreed to persuade her of the meeting.
   ( ) Ranjana made her parents believe that the meeting would be a good thing.

2. There can be nothing worse than to realize that your marriage will put a complete end to all your freedom.
   ( ) There can be nothing worse than to give up your freedom and marry.
   ( ) At worst you will see that your marriage will restrict your freedom.
   ( ) Things are at their worst when you understand that your marriage will definitely end your freedom.
   ( ) You feel worst at the idea of marrying someone who oppresses your freedom.

A 3 Explain in your own words! Write in your notebook.

1. Ranjana's arranged marriage
2. the man of her choice
3. a boarding school
4. a wedding day
5. they will be free to do something

A 4 Find a synonymous expression for the bold words. Write the complete sentences in your notebook.

1. She was **educated** at a boarding school.
2. He's a man she **hardly** knows.
3. I choose a husband **by myself.**
4. She saw her **husband-to-be.**
5. **I'm against** arranged marriages.
6. I've **argued** for a long time.
7. **I'm used** to being away from home.
8. You know **nothing can come of it.**
9. **I intend** to write to him.
10. **I'm certain** of one thing.
11. **Maybe** I would meet someone.

A 5 Give the feminine equivalent of the following words.

1. husband ____________
2. headmaster ____________
3. bridegroom ____________
4. widower ____________
5. actor ____________
6. hero ____________
7. nephew ____________

A 6 Word building: To which of the following parts of words can you add 1. the syllable "in-", 2. the syllable "re-", 3. both syllables?

-tend, -sist, -form, -ceive, -port, -clude

Grammatik

A 7 Auxiliaries: Fill in "may" or "might".

1. Her parents said that she ________________ go to see him.
2. She saw him only once, she ________________ as well marry a stranger.
3. Come what ________________ , she'll always obey her parents.
4. If she sees him, she ________________ love him.
5. If he came, she ________________ see him.

A 8 Rewrite the following sentences using "may". Leave out "perhaps".

1. Perhaps he comes.
2. Perhaps he will have arrived by now.
3. Perhaps he is working.
4. Perhaps I have been sleeping.
5. Perhaps you are right.
6. Perhaps he has lived in India.
7. Perhaps he was waiting for us.
8. Perhaps they were there.

A 9 Fill in: "can" or "may".

1. It ________________ rain.
2. ________________ you speak Hindu?
3. ________________ you remember her name?
4. This story ________________ or ________________ not be true.

A 10 Fill in the corresponding forms of "to be able to".

1. I ________________________ to do it before he came back.
2. Since his operation he ________________________ to walk.
3. Their baby ________________________ to walk in a few weeks.
4. Although the busdriver was badly hurt he ____________________ to explain what had happened.
5. He can't drive a car because he's broken his leg, but in a few weeks, he ________________________ to drive again.

A 11 Fill in: "mustn't" or "needn't".

1. It's warm outside, you _____________________ put on a coat.
2. You _____________________ speak with your mouth full.
3. Pupils _____________________ be late for school.
4. You _____________________ drive so fast, there's plenty of time.
5. The doctor said I _____________________ smoke so much.
6. The doctor said I _________________ stay in hospital any longer.
7. You _____________________ take a taxi, you can go by bus.

3.5 Levi's Blue Jeans

It all started with a single pair of trousers made of strong, thick cloth in the days of the Californian gold rush and a hard-working, industrious immigrant named Levi ['liːvaɪ] Strauss.
Over the years, the business founded on that pair of trousers has generated more wealth than any gold seeker ever took out of the gold mines: Up to now, more than 90,000,000 pairs of jeans have been sold. And they have been sold almost unchanged for more than one hundred years.
Levi Strauss was of German origin. his birthplace is Buttenheim, a village near Bamberg in Bavaria. When his father died, he emigrated with

his mother to New York where his two stepbrothers ran a shop which sold needles, pins, scissors and cloth. For a short time, he joined his two brothers in their business, but soon, he wanted to be his own boss, and he set up a business.
In 1850, the 20-year-old Bavarian immigrant to the US boarded a New York sailing ship bound for California to sell his goods to miners. He intended to sell rough canvas for tents and wagon cover.
Once ashore, a gold seeker asked him: "What have you brought with you on the boat?" "These rolls of canvas here", Levi pointed to his rolls of strong cloth. "You'd have brought trousers", said the miner. "You'd better sell trousers." "Do you need many trousers here?", asked the surprised newcomer. "Our trousers wear out, they don't last, they wear badly", the miner replied.
That's when Levi Strauss got his great idea. He took a roll of canvas and had a tailor make it into a pair of trousers for the digger. And it made durable work trousers for his new friend.

Soon, other miners wanted to buy the same trousers and Levi wrote to his brothers for a supply of heavy cloth. They sent him a thick cotton cloth from France, known as "serge de Nîmes" (Nîmes, town in Southern France), later shortened to "denim".
When some of the miners complained that the seams of the pockets were not strong enough, Levi had them made stronger by copper rivets. Thus, the miners' demands were satisfied.
As Levi did not like the colour of the cloth, he had it dyed blue violet. That was in the 1860s, and today, the trousers are made exactly as they were then.

Within a few years, the fashion of Levi's spread from California to the East Coast. Sales rocketed. Levi's were worn not only by miners and cowboys, but by farmers, workers and clerks. Today, however, Levi's real popularity is among young people.

Words from the text you may not know:

to board	an Bord gehen
canvas	Segeltuch
cloth	Tuch
to complain	sich beklagen
copper	Kupfer
cotton	Baumwolle
digger	Goldgräber
durable	haltbar
to dye	färben
to found on	gründen auf
to generate	hervorbringen
goods	Waren
industrious	fleißig
to join	sich anschließen
miner	Bergmann
needle	Nähnadel
pin	Stecknadel
reasonable	vernünftig
rivet	Niete
to rocket	in die Höhe schnellen
rough	grob
scissors	Schere
seam	Naht
to shorten	abkürzen
to spread	sich ausbreiten
supply	Lieferung, Nachschub
tailor	Schneider
to take up	anfangen
wagon cover	Wagenplane
wealth	Reichtum

Fragen zum Text

A 1 Answer in complete sentences.

1. Why did lots of people go to California in the middle of the 19th century?
2. Which was more profitable: selling jeans or finding gold?
3. Is there a big difference between the jeans which you can buy today and the jeans sold during the Californian gold rush?
4. What kind of work did Levi's stepbrothers do?
5. What did Levi plan to do in California?
6. Why can we say that the miners' trousers were not of high quality?
7. Why were some of the miners dissatisfied with the jeans?

Wortschatz

A 2 Complete the sentences with the given words.

1. cloth – cloths – clothes – clothing

   Where did you buy these elegant ____________________? –

   I bought them in a boutique.

   Is the ____________________ of the tent waterproof?

   When I was in Italy, I bought some articles of ____________________.

   The waiters laid new table____________________ on the tables.

2. industrial – industrious

   There is a lot of air pollution in the ____________________ areas.

   This pupil works hard, he's very ____________________.

3. shop – business

   My friend is in the car __________________ , he sells a car nearly

   every day.

Betty is in the wool ______________ , she's buying wool for a new pullover.

In December, before Christmas, ______________ booms, and the ______________ are full of people.

4. found – founded

It was the Dutch who ______________ New York.

The immigrants ______________ a new colony.

In 1848, gold was ______________ in California.

5. thick – fat

There were no jeans wide enough for the ______________ gentleman.

John was eating a ______________ slice of bread.

Is your friend thin? – No, he's rather ______________.

6. immigrants – emigrants

Every day, illegal ______________ from Mexico try to cross the borders of the US.

People who leave their country to live in another one are ______________.

A 3 Complete the sentences with the given words.

1. die – dye

The girl wanted to __________ her hair green and yellow.

Lots of trees __________ of acid rain.

2. bring – take

Taxi please! Can you __________ me to the airport?

He will __________ her a bunch of flowers.

Please, ____________ your dictionary to every lesson.

How many friends will you __________ to my party?

3. wear – carry

She could hardly ____________ her heavy suitcase.

Are you going to ____________ this crazy shirt?

Which shoes do you ____________ in your bag?

4. roll – role

What is the _______________ of school in our society?

What do you need this _______________ of paper for?

She bought four _______________ at the baker's.

5. price – prize

I'd like to know the _____________ of this car.

She won the first _____________ in the 100 metres.

John is a good athlete, he always gets _____________.

I can't pay that _____________.

A 4 Find the corresponding adjectives or nouns.

adjective	noun
	wealth
	origin
surprised	
	France
	popularity
fashionable	

A 5 Find the opposites!

1. a thick cloth
2. he emigrated
3. they wear badly (sich rasch abnutzen)
4. other miners
5. later

A 6 Find expressions with meanings similar to the bold words from the text.

1. **it all started** with
2. **up to** now
3. **almost** unchanged
4. with **a single** pair of trousers
5. came the **reply**
6. what they **desire**
7. **in the days of** the Californian gold rush

A 7 Complete the following text!

Levi Strauss was ______________ in Buttenheim not ______________ from Bamberg. After his father's ______________ , he ______________ Germany and went to New York. He wanted to ______________ a businessman. In 1848, gold had been ______________ in California, and thousands of people who wanted to ______________ rich rushed to the gold mines. Levi Strauss, however, did not want to ______________ gold, he wanted to ______________ his goods to the ______________. He was a typical self______________ man. His ______________ came true: Towards the end of his ______________ – he ______________ in 1902 – he was one of the richest men in America.

A 8 Find the word in the text for ...

1. a long, thin piece of steel with a point at one end and a little hole at the other,
2. a man who has others working for or under him,
3. a shelter made of a thick piece of cloth held up by strong sticks,
4. to be dressed in,
5. to say that something or someone is not as it should be,
6. to change the colour of a cloth,
7. the exchange of something for money.

Grammatik

A 9 Complete the verb forms.

simple present	simple past	past participle	-ing-form
go	went	gone	going
	founded		
	found		
seek			
	died		
	dyed		
wear			
		spread	

Beachte die Präposition von "to die": „sterben ***an*** *einer Krankheit" – "to die* ***of*** *an illness"!*

Tipp!

A 10 Put the fifth paragraph into indirect speech. Write the complete sentences in your notebook. Begin with "Once ashore, a gold seeker asked him what he ..."

A 11 Complete the sentences from the text changing the passive into the active voice.

1. Up to now, they ____________________ more than 90,000,000 pairs of jeans.
2. ... today, they ______________ the trousers exactly as they were then.
3. Not only miners and cowboys, but also farmers, workers and clerks ________________ Levi's.

A 12 Complete the sentences from the text changing the active into the passive voice.

1. "Do you need many trousers here?"
2. They sent him a thick cotton cloth from France.

A 13 Guided writing.

1. The gold seeker, to whom Levi Strauss had given the first pair of blue jeans, told friends about the quality of his new trousers. What did he say? Write two or three sentences.
2. What did some of the miners say who were not satisfied with the quality of their jeans? Write two or three sentences.
3. Levi Strauss made up the trademark himself. Describe the picture in the middle of the patch. What did Levi Strauss want to symbolize by this picture? Write two or three sentences.

A 14 Guided dialogue: Put in the missing words.

Betty: ______________________________ trousers?

Sally: Yes, I like them very much. I've never seen such trousers.

__________________________________?

Betty: In a department store in the town centre.

Sally: __________________________________?

Betty: No, they weren't. I bought them at a reasonable price.

A 15 Du bist in einem großen Kaufhaus in London und möchtest dir Jeans kaufen. Beachte, dass "jeans" ein Pluralwort ist, du musst also auch die Pluralformen der Pronomen "they", "them", "ones" verwenden, auch wenn es sich nur um eine einzige Hose handelt! Sage der Verkäuferin bzw. frage sie ...

1. ob sie gelbe Jeans hat,
2. dass du Größe XL hast,
3. wo du sie anprobieren kannst,
4. dass sie dir gefallen, aber zu weit sind,
5. ob sie eine kleinere hat, eine Größe kleiner,
6. dass die kleinere dir passt. Du wirst sie nehmen.

A 16 Deine Freundin/dein Freund hat ein neues Kleid/einen neuen Pullover an. Mache ihr/ihm ein Kompliment.

1. Es/er gefällt dir sehr gut.
2. Sie/er sieht gut aus in ihrem neuen Kleid/seinem neuen Pullover.
3. Es/er steht ihr/ihm gut.
4. Die Farbe passt gut zu ihrem/seinem Haar.

3.6 Coca-Cola

Some people consider Coca-Cola a joke – they are mistaken: a beverage of which forty thousand bottles are sold a second cannot be a joke. Coca-Cola is not only a monumental business, it is one of the principal symbols of the American way of life.

Atlanta, Georgia, 1885. Dr. John Pemberton, a pharmacist, was experimenting in his laboratory to find remedies for coughs, headaches, rheumatism or whatever could help people to restore their health. When he put a few leaves from the South American coca bush into a brown, sugary syrup, he invented Coca-Cola. Business with the soft drink grew rapidly, and it became the most important American product of the 20th century.

In early 1945, a group of German prisoners of war disembarked in a small port in New Jersey. When one of them pointed to a Coca-Cola sign on a nearby building, they began to gesticulate excitedly and to talk among themselves. An army officer asked for an explanation from a prisoner who spoke English. “We are surprised”, came the answer, “that you have Coca-Cola here, too.”

Coca-Cola managers like to tell this story as a proof that there were no barriers to the expansion of the drink, even Nazi Germany could not stop this world-famous refreshment. Indeed, up to 1994, Coca-Cola had found its way into 189 countries all over the world, even into Communist China.

What are the reasons for this astounding success? The first reason is the fact that Coke has been easy to get. The managers organized markets with thousands of vending machines in factories, offices, and sports arenas. The drink can be bought in the shop round the corner and in big supermarkets, in fastfood places, and in first class restaurants.
Secondly, Coca-Cola is not too expensive, it is not only for those who live a life of luxury. Those who are poor can afford it, too. Coke is kept cheap for cash-poor consumers in the Third World, the new, profitable market.
The third and most important reason is Coca-Cola's successful advertising: attractive, smiling people make you think of good times, friends, leisure, success and being "in".

Coke pays large sums for ads in newspapers, magazines, films, sports fields, and at car races. In 1988, the company spent about 80 million dollars on TV programs reporting the Olympic Games. Coke's publicity experts have managed to win prominent people: sportsmen, film stars and even presidents of the US.
Coke's success is unparalleled, this American drink has conquered the globe. However, it is also severely criticised. It is called a symbol of the aggressive American politics. It is said to show the "Americanization" of the world. It illustrates capitalism: the poor are exploited, the rich get richer every day. Nevertheless, no other drink has ever enjoyed

such world-wide popularity, no other drink has been so quickly accepted by so many different people in so many different countries. An American travelling across the Sahara asked the driver of the Land-Rover when they would leave civilisation behind. The driver, an Arab, did not know the expression "leave civilisation behind". The American tried to explain: "It's the place where you can't buy any Coca-Cola". The driver understood and shook his head. "Never", he said and pointed to a sign which appeared behind the next sand dune. It was an advertisement for Coca-Cola.

Words from the text you may not know:

advertising	Werbung
astounding	verblüffend
to banish	verbannen
to be mistaken	im Irrtum sein
about	über
beverage	Getränk
cash-poor	knapp bei Kasse
to connect with	verbinden mit
to conquer	erobern
consumer	Verbraucher
cough	Husten
to disembark	von Bord gehen, ausschiffen
to exploit	ausbeuten
globe	Weltkugel
health	Gesundheit
leisure	Muße, Freizeit
luxury	Luxus
pharmacist	Apotheker
proof (Pl.: proofs)	Beweis
publicity	Werbung
remedy	Heilmittel, Arznei
to restore	wiederherstellen
sugary	zuckrig
unparalleled	unvergleichlich, beispiellos
vending machine	Warenautomat

Fragen zum Text

A 1 Answer in complete sentences.

1. How many bottles of Coca-Cola do people buy per minute all over the world?
2. What does a pharmacist do?
3. What did Dr. Pemberton add to the syrup?
4. Why were the German prisoners astonished?
5. Which expressions in the text tells you that you can buy Coca-Cola on every continent?
6. What do you need to buy Coca-Cola from a vending machine?
7. Which prominent personalities advertised Coca-Cola?
8. Why is it especially important for a company to advertise on TV programs reporting the Olympic Games?
9. Which economic system is mentioned in the text?
10. What is the critics' opinion of Coca-Cola?

Wortschatz

A 2 Which paraphrase or definition fits best? Mark the correct expression with a cross.

1. to be mistaken:	( )	to miss taking something
	( )	to correct a mistake
	( )	to have a wrong idea
2. principal:	( )	the first and most important
	( )	a little prince
	( )	an important principle
3. a pharmacist:	( )	a person working in a company
	( )	a person taking drugs
	( )	a person qualified to prepare and sell medicines

4. to disembark:
( ) to stop a dog barking
( ) to go on shore from a ship
( ) to unload a sailing ship

5. to afford:
( ) to earn money
( ) to save money
( ) to have enough money for

6. leisure:
( ) time free from work
( ) time passing quickly
( ) time people spend at home

A 3 Complete the definitions using words from the text.

1. A ______________________ is a building where things are made, usually by machines.
2. ______________________ is something very expensive that you do not really need.
3. A ______________________ is a thin book which comes out every week or month with articles and pictures.
4. An ________________ is someone who knows a lot about a particular object.
5. A ____________________ is someone who is famous and popular.

A 4 Find the words with the opposite meaning (antonyms).

1. health ____________
2. rapidly ____________
3. war ____________
4. future ____________
5. nearby ____________
6. excitedly ____________
7. enemy ____________
8. expensive ____________
9. leisure ____________
10. success ____________

A 5 Word building: Which verb goes with the following nouns?

1. a product ____________
2. an explanation ____________
3. a proof ____________
4. a success ____________
5. an advertisement [əd'vɜːtɪsmənt] ____________

A 6 Which noun goes with the following adjectives?

1. important ____________
2. excited ____________
3. poor ____________
4. profitable ____________
5. attractive ____________
6. aggressive ____________
7. rich ____________
8. different ____________

A 7 Write down the sentence of the expression in the text which tells you that ...

1. Dr. Pemberton wanted to help sick people,
2. more and more Coca-Cola was sold,
3. an officer wanted to know why the German prisoners of war were so upset,
4. Coca-Cola spends much money on advertising.

A 8 Complete the following sentences.

1. The baby wanted something to eat and drink because he was _______________ and _______________.

2. At a pharmacy, you can buy _______________ for most _______________.
3. The man or the woman who _______________ meals in restaurants are called _______________ or _______________.
4. _______________ serve in the army, _______________ serve in the navy.
5. He is a successful businessman who makes a lot of _______________ by _______________ lots of goods.

A 9 Put in "discover" or "invent".

1. This man _______________ed a machine that had never been thought of before.
2. The managers _______________ed a new market in the Third World.
3. Do you know who _______________ed the vending machines? – It was the Romans.

Achte auf den Unterschied: "to discover" heißt „(etwas bereits Vorhandenes) entdecken", "to invent" dagegen „(etwas Neues) erfinden, sich ausdenken".

Tipp!

A 10 Put in "story" or "history".

1. The boy came late and he invented a ____________________ for an excuse.
2. ____________________ teaches us what happened in the past.
3. Do you like this ____________________?
4. Do you like ____________________?

Beachte: "story" heißt „Geschichte" im Sinne von „Erzählung", „Bericht", "history" dagegen hat die Bedeutung „Chronik", „Wissenschaft von der Vergangenheit"!

Tipp!

A 11 Put in "travel", "drive" or "run".

1. Does this bus ____________________ on Sundays?
2. Did you ____________________ by train?
3. Did you ____________________ the car yourself?

Der Unterschied: "to travel (by)" bedeutet „fahren (mit einem Verkehrsmittel)", "to drive" „(selbst mit einem Fahrzeug) fahren", "to run" „verkehren", „in Betrieb sein".

Tipp!

A 12 Put in "delicious" or "delicate".

1. Can they solve this ____________________ problem?
2. The poor boy is in ____________________ health.
3. The dessert was simply ____________________.

Vorsicht, ein falscher Freund! "delicate" heißt „fein", „empfindlich" oder auch „heikel", "delicious" dagegen bedeutet „köstlich", „schmackhaft"!

Tipp!

A 13 Paraphrases: Rewrite the sentences from the text using other expressions for the bold words.

1. Coca-Cola managers **like to tell** this story **as a proof** that there were no barriers.
2. Coke is kept cheap for **cash-poor** consumers in the **Third World.**
3. Coke's publicity experts have **managed to** win prominent people.

Grammatik

A 14 The indefinite article "a" or "an"? Complete the sentences.

1. You usually lose money whey you play on _____ one-armed bandit in a casino.
2. I think the butler is _____ honest man.
3. At some British schools pupils must still wear _____ uniform.
4. Can you lend me _____ umbrella, please?
5. That's _____ useful idea.
6. Slovenia is _____ European country.

3 Leseverständnis

A 15 Fill in the indefinite article if necessary.

1. My brother is _____ car mechanic.
2. Is there _____ milk in the fridge?
3. What _____ terrible weather!
4. Monika wants to become _____ stewardess.
5. What _____ terrible boy!

A 16 The s-genitive: Put in “‘”, “s‘” or “‘s”.

1. Where are our guests_____ drinks?
2. The ladies_____ glasses are empty.
3. The children_____ lemonades are too cold.
4. James_____ job is hard.
5. Have you read today_____ paper?
6. Whose car is that? – It’s my parents_____.
7. You can buy it at the chemist_____.

A 17 If-clauses: Complete the sentences!

1. If you drink too much lemonade, you (get) _______________ fat.
2. If the managers (work) _______________ harder, the company will be more successful.
3. If they advertised, they (sell) _________________________ more.
4. If it (be) _______________ hotter, we would drink more.
5. If I (have) _________________________ your number, I would have telephoned you.

A 18 Rewrite these sentences. Begin each sentence with "if".

1. She didn't give me her address, so I can't send her a birthday card.
2. I didn't have enough money, so I didn't invite her for a drink.
3. They didn't take a taxi, therefore they arrived later.
4. They won't visit the museum because they haven't got enough time.
5. The weather was so bad that we stayed in the hotel all the time.
6. Take this medicine. You'll soon feel well again.

A 19 Put in "if" or "when".

1. You'll drop your glass, ___________ you aren't more careful.
2. ___________ you're thirsty, you'll find something to drink in the fridge.
3. It always rained in our holidays ___________ we wanted to go swimming.
4. ___________ I arrived at the station, I could not find my ticket.

A 20 Fill in the missing prepositions.

1. to talk: Who's the girl he's talking ___________? What subject is he talking ___________?
2. symbol: McDonald's is a symbol ___________ the American way of life.
3. money: He paid a lot of money ________ this old car. Don't spend all your money __________ sweets. I must save money _________ a holiday. He has an account ________ a bank, and he pays ________ a small amount ________ money every month.

Tipp!

Achte auf die Präpositionen:

1. ***mit** jemandem sprechen – to talk **to** somebody (selten: "with"), aber:*
   ***über** etwas sprechen – to talk **about** something*
2. *to be a symbol **of** something – ein Symbol **für** etwas sein*
3. *Geld ausgeben **für** – to spend money **on***
   *Geld sparen **auf/für** – to save money **for***

A 21 Complete the sentences using "for" or "of".

1. Your parents are proud ________ you.
2. Would you care ________ a drink?
3. This drink smells ________ medicine.
4. Peter is going to apply ________ a position in this firm.

A 22 Guided writing: Ask questions!

1. One bottle is 30p.
2. I bought the drinks at the supermarket.
3. Coca-Cola was invented in the year 1885.
4. We'll meet at ten o'clock.
5. This drink smells of lemon.

A 23 Eating in a restaurant.
Complete the dialogue.

1. What ________________________ for dinner? – ______________
   __________ a soup first.
2. ________________________ fish or meat? – I prefer fish.

3. Would you ____________________ to drink? – Yes, a ____________ mineral water, please.
4. How ________________________? – They have got two kinds of cheese.
5. Did you ________ the waiter ____________ bill? – Yes, I did.
6. This is quite ______ good restaurant, ________ it? – Indeed, ________.

A 24 Sage deinem Freund oder deiner Freundin ...

1. dass du zu dick wirst, wenn du zu viel Cola trinkst.
2. dass du dir ein Fahrrad kaufen würdest, wenn du genügend Geld hättest.
3. dass du mehr Getränke für deine Geburtstagsparty gekauft hättest, wenn du mehr Geld gehabt hättest.

Übersetzungen aus der Fremdsprache

Tipps zur Arbeitstechnik

1. Beginne nicht gleich mit dem Übersetzen der Überschrift und des ersten Satzes, sondern lies erst den ganzen Text einmal aufmerksam durch. Halte dich beim ersten Durchlesen nicht zu lange bei unbekannten Wörtern auf. Mache dir klar, was das Hauptthema des Textes ist, z.B. Umweltschutz, Jugendprobleme, Rassenkonflikte usw.

2. Jeder Text enthält mehr oder weniger unbekannte Wörter. Wie kannst du ihren Sinn herausfinden?
   Nehmen wir das Wort "magnifying". Mit großer Wahrscheinlichkeit hast du es noch nie gehört und kannst es demnach nicht ins Deutsche übersetzen. Versuche, die Bedeutung aus dem Satzzusammenhang zu erschließen!

   Beispiel: Das Wort "magnifying" steht in folgendem Satz:
   "To read John's small handwriting, you almost need a magnifying glass."

   Aus dem Zusammenhang geht hervor: "Magnifying" hat etwas mit „vergrößern" zu tun: Um Johns kleine Handschrift zu lesen, brauchst du ein bestimmtes Glas, d.h. ein Vergrößerungsglas.

   Wenn dir ein bestimmtes Wort aber trotzdem nicht klar ist, kannst du es selbstverständlich in einem einsprachigen Lexikon nachschlagen.

3. Häufig klagen Schüler, dass sie zwar wissen, was ein Satz bedeutet, dass sie aber den Satz nicht in gutem Deutsch wiedergeben können. Versuche doch mal Folgendes:

   Übersetze einen problematischen Satz ungefähr wörtlich und übertrage dann diese Rohübersetzung in ordentliches Deutsch. Dazu solltest du die Rohübersetzung auf ein Blatt Papier schreiben – wenn du die Bedeutung des Satzes vor Augen hast, fällt es dir leichter, dich auf das nächste Problem, gutes Deutsch, zu konzentrieren.

Ein Beispiel: Das Thema des Textes ist „Zeitungen“:
“Even more newspapers are sold at weekends when you have enough time to sit and read for hours.”

Die Rohübersetzung könnte lauten:
„Sogar mehr Zeitungen werden verkauft an Wochenenden, wenn du genügend Zeit hast zum Sitzen und zum Lesen für Stunden.“

Mit diesem Rohmaterial vor Augen fällt es nun leichter, den Satz in normales Deutsch umzuformen:
„Noch mehr Zeitungen werden an Wochenenden verkauft, wenn man genügend Zeit hat, stundenlang dazusitzen und zu lesen.“

4.1 Christopher Columbus

Since 1484, Columbus had been trying to persuade the rulers of Portugal and Spain to finance this project to find a new route to India. Finally Columbus gained the support of the Spanish monarchs Ferdinand and Isabella and the great voyage of discovery began on August 3rd, 1492.

From a copy of Columbus's diary we know that the crew were unhappy about sailing off into the limitless sea. By October 8th the crew wanted to turn back, but Columbus told them if they hadn't landed within three days, they should cut off his head and return to Europe.

When Columbus and his men finally reached the Caribbean Islands, the search for gold and precious stones began. 32 weeks later, Columbus arrived back home, without having lost a single man at sea. Although some people denied that Columbus had got as far as India, he was invited to the Spanish court where he was received with great honours.

On his second voyage Columbus took 17 ships, 1,500 sailors, soldiers and settlers with him. On board they also had plants, animals and tools for a permanent settlement.

4.2 Immigration Today

Each week 2,500 immigrants arrive at J. F. Kennedy airport. These immigrants come for the same reasons that brought people to the US in the past: to escape oppression and to find a better life for themselves and for their children. But today, they come from other parts of the world.

Whereas up to 1950 the majority came from Europe, today's newcomers emigrate from Asia, the Caribbean, and Latin America. The new Americans get the so-called "green card", which is a working permit, and which entitles them to permanent residence.

Of course, many immigrants enter without permission. Roberto for instance. I met him in New York. He was dressed in a thin pullover on a cold January afternoon, he was selling Mexican sweets, earning 35 dollars a day. In Mexico City he had been a car mechanic, but in New York, without a green card, he could find work only as a vendor. A "travel agent" had led him across the border by night and put him on a plane to New York – for 700 dollars, which Roberto had borrowed from a relative.

Congress attempts to stop such illegal immigration. A law was passed which punishes employers who hire workers without documents. However, illegal immigrants keep coming, like Roberto, who told me: "I like America. I make money, and I feel good here."

4.3 What The National Trust Has For You

If you think the National Trust's main concern is with country houses and their contents, then you're only partly right. For besides the Trust's 250 historic buildings it also preserves – for us all, and for all time – gardens and landscaped parks, countryside including woods and downland, lakes, mountains and half our finest remaining coastline, prehistoric and Roman sites, relics of our industrial past, more than a thousand farms – even forty traditional villages.

Add to these its 165 shops, its welcoming restaurants offering local meals, its country parks and nature reserves, and its holiday cottages and summer festivals, then we can begin to appreciate the richness of the British heritage that's owned by the National Trust.

To keep all this going costs over £50 million a year. But the Trust is in no way a government agency. Receiving no regular official funding, it's kept alive by the private sector – by ordinary people like you and me. If you want to help, the best way is by joining the Trust.

National Trust houses offer fun and fascination for everyone and not only provide a way of making your membership work but also let you see how we use income from members. Whatever your choice of leisure activity, the National Trust has something to offer you.

4.4 Lawnmowers That Do Not Cut Grass

It's a rainy Saturday morning in a suburb not far from Sheffield. A middle-aged gentleman is trying to start a lawnmower, despite the rain. Again and again he pulls the rope and finally he manages to start the machine's engine. The gentleman puts on his crash helmet, gets onto the seat and off he roars.

He's driving to a large pasture not far from his terraced house. About sixty drivers with roaring engines are waiting for him. There are clouds of smoke and a brain-rattling noise.

At nine o'clock the lawnmower race begins. It is an endurance race which lasts for twelve hours. In this race not a blade of grass gets cut, since the mowers' blades are removed for safety reasons.

Along the track you find an atmosphere like that of a campsite: caravans and tents, hot dog and ice cream stands, noisy children running around in the mud and mothers doing the dirty dishes in the open air under big umbrellas, fathers lying in deckchairs and dogs sniffing at barbecues.

The race is organized by the BLMRA, the "British Lawn Mower Racing Association" which is recognized by Britain's Royal Automobile Club. It takes place nearly every weekend at some farmer's field.

Of course, the BLMRA has strict rules. Three pages of fine-print dictate everything from the shape of the seat to the number of stops at the pits. The most important rule is that the mowers must have been manufactured and sold to mow home lawns, not golf courses or public parks. A BBC commentator observed during a telecast of the twelve-hour endurance race: "This is a classic British sport: played by fanatics, under absurd rules, generally in the rain."

Lösungen

Bei manchen Aufgaben, etwa zu den Zusammenfassungen, zum Textverständnis oder zur Übersetzung aus dem Englischen können die angegebenen Lösungen nur Musterlösungen sein. Wenn deine Lösungen nicht so ausführlich sind, so ist das nicht schlimm: Vergleiche sie mit den angegebenen und überlege, ob deine auch richtig sind und worin sie sich unterscheiden.

1. Wiederholung – Revision

1. is visited, 2. largest – most exciting, 3. you can be seen, 4. has been given – have seen, 5. stand, 6. was very badly damaged, 7. could be saved, 8. finest, 9. have been crowned, 10. are buried, 11. used, 12. contains – including, 13. is flying, 14. means, 15. are attracted, 16. held, 17. led, 18. arrives, 19. Do you know, 20. are kept, 21. had been, 22. can easily see, 23. have been closed down, 24. had to, 25. to live, 26. would have enjoyed staying, 27. are being built, 28. come, 29. won't recognize. 30. will have completely changed, 31. didn't want – was

2. Übungen zur Zusammenfassung – Summary Writing

2.1 Canada's Native People

Canadian Inuit and Indians are proud of having been their country's first inhabitants and of having stuck to their habitual ways of life.
Only recently have technological progress and cultural influences from the South made these Northerners adopt some advantages of modern society.
The revival of interest in their aboriginal art has boosted their self-esteem. Consequently, they even dare claim property rights.
(62 words)

2.2 Television Programmes

TV programmes can roughly be classified like this: those designed to inform and to set their viewers thinking and those whose only purpose is entertainment.

Both kinds of programmes are equally valid and everyone can choose the ones he or she likes. But are all entertainment programmes really worth watching?
(50 words)

2.3 Modern Magic
In Shakespearean times circling the earth within a few minutes' time was a utopian dream, and instant communication inconceivable. Nowadays the latter has become reality, and TV and radio sets are ubiquitous. Therefore millions of viewers and listeners can zap to scenes anywhere in the world, which makes them more powerful than the legendary Aladdin. But do they always wield their power cleverly?
(63 words)

3. Leseverständnis – Reading Comprehension

3.1 The Big Apple

1

1. The Statue of Liberty reminds us of the French and the American Revolution.
2. New York originally had a Dutch name because it was founded by Dutch merchants and immigrants who gave it the name New Amsterdam.
3. Many people have left their countries because of the poor social and working conditions there. The new immigrants are attracted by the New World represented to them by the modern buildings of steel and glass of Manhattan, for example. They hope to find a new life with better jobs and opportunities for themselves and their children.
4. In past centuries people emigrated to America to find religious freedom, to escape from overcrowded Europe and build up a new life in a land of better opportunities, to seek their fortune by digging for gold, and for many other reasons.
5. In New York you will find a great contrast between Times Square with its huge advertisement illumination flashing on and off round the clock and dirty, poverty-stricken slum districts. The inhabitants of New York provide us with a great contrast, too. Not only are there whites, blacks and Hispanic people but also thousands of people of other nationalities and races.

6. The houses of a slum district are mainly dirty, unsanitary old buildings whose supplies of water, electricity and heating are very often inadequate. And in such areas where poverty is at home, crime flourishes.

2 1. In New York, people of different nations are transformed into Americans. 2. You are confused when you see the outline of the skyscrapers against the sky.

3 1. We came near the harbour. 2. We came in view of the statue. 3. The Dutch established a colony. 4. The Dutch were the first founders. 5. There is an uninterrupted flow of people. 6. The greater number of these people are poor. 7. It's an immense problem. 8. They live with not enough water. 9. It's not far off Broadway.

4 1. a sight which is well-known, 2. a city in which you find elements from many different countries of the world, 3. a building which rises up like a tower

5

to radiate	radiation	radiant
to attract	attraction	attractive
to fear	fear	fearful
to vitalize	vitality	vital
–	energy	energetic
to advertise	advertisement	advertising
to originate	origin/originality	original
–	importance	important
to differ	difference	different

6 1. fearful, fearless, harmful, harmless, useful, useless, careful, careless, helpful, helpless, 2. needless, restless, 3. thankful, successful, forgetful

7 **list 1:** the Statue of Liberty, the Empire State Building, the United States of America, the President of the US, during the night, throughout the night, in the sea, with the help of

list 2: Manhattan Island, North America, Israel, Southern Europe, President Nixon, Times Square, Broadway, by night, at night, capitalism, to go by sea, in memory of, at first sight, in public, on condition that

8 1. –, 2. the, 3. –, 4. the, 5. –, 6. the, 7. the, 8. –, 9. –, 10. the, 11. –, 12. the

9 1. They paid twice the price. 2. Both the boys were late. 3. I did it in half the time. 4. He asked for double the amount. 5. All the people were shouting. 6. The faster people drive, the more accidents will occur.

10 **list 1:** I'm in a hurry, she has a headache, he is a Frenchman, he took a seat, there is a lot of time, as a rule

list 2: they made way for the king, there is plenty of time, there is good news, she took notice of him, he will arrive in time

11 1. artists, 2. some bottles, 3. Americans, 4. some nice books, 5. engineers, 6. good players, 7. some sandwiches, 8. some voices, 9. pretty girls

12 1. A rainy day – we had one day, 2. One bar of chocolate a day, 3. A knife – one knife, 4. need a sheet – thank you, one sheet, 5. is a friend – is one of

13 1. I have never seen such a building before. 2. I bought half a pound. 3. It costs 6p a dozen. 4. Many a sailor never returned. 5. This is quite a good thing.

14 1. at a loss, 2. At times, 3. at work, 4. at war with, 5. at once, 6. At last, 7. at once, 8. At present

15 sea – see, steel – steal, whole – hole, new – knew, hour – our

16 approach, apologize, immigrant, emigrant, assimilate, abundant, address, disappear, imagine, imitate, immense, immediately, innumerable, possess, opinion

3.2 The American Frontier

1 1. In this context the term "frontier" means the area where the first settlers struggled against the wilderness, the forces of nature, and the Indians. The pioneers went on pushing this frontier westward, as more and more settlers arrived and thus more land was needed, until in 1890 they reached their most westward frontier, the Pacific Ocean.

2. The pioneers were confronted with many dangers. In the hostile wilderness where they lived they could but rarely rely on military protection. Living in this wilderness where they were deprived of a lot of things they had taken for granted in Europe, they could easily fall ill and need a doctor, it took days to reach one.
3. The proverb "necessity is the mother of invention" means that if you are in real need of something and cannot obtain it you will find a way of inventing the thing required yourself. Necessity makes people resourceful and inventive.
4. America is one of the most highly developed countries in the world, which makes her a great industrial and economic power. She leads the world in science and technology. Last but not least she has great political influence.

2 1. They were compelled to gain new abilities for themselves. 2. Europeans often find that they are over-optimistic.

3 1. same, 2. decreasing, 3. weak, 4. friendly, 5. the worst

4 1. to mean, 2. to expand, 3. to invent, 4. to produce, 5. to solve, 6. to rely on

5 1. in general every day use, 2. it means, 3. they grew/got too small, 4. an increasing number of, 5. they had arrived at, 6. courageous, 7. they were confronted with, 8. they were taken away/had to do without, 9. to master difficulties, 10. untiring energy

6 1. speech, 2. wilderness, 3. growth, 4. strength, 5. hostility, 6. survival, 7. essence, 8. necessity

7 self-reliance, self-service, self-control, self-protection, self-respect, self-interest, self-made

8 1. homework, workbook, 2. log house, housewife, country house, household, 3. birthday, daybreak, pay day, daytime, 4. paper bag, newspaper, paper money, writing paper, 5. headmaster, masterpiece, schoolmaster, master stroke

9 buildings, meanings, paintings, drawings

10 1. In vain had the Indians attacked the camp. 2. Seldom has there been a peaceful time. 3. No sooner had the settlements become too small than the settlers moved westward. 4. Hardly had they arrived than they had to fight. 5. At no time was there peace.

11 1. They sent it to them. 2. He gave it to him. 3. He bought it for her. 4. I described it to him. 5. He took it off. 6. She put it on. 7. He laid it down.

12 1. He wants to know where the settlers are going to. 2. Can you tell me where I must go? 3. Show me where the gold is hidden. 4. Tell me why they are leaving the settlements.

13 1. a) The settler lent his neighbour his axe. b) The settler lent his axe to his neighbour who lived 20 miles away.
2. a) He showed his friends the gold. b) He showed the gold to all his curious friends and neighbours.
3. a) He explained me his plan. b) He explained his plan to everyone who wanted to know it.

14 1. starts/departs, 2. Who is, 3. Keep away, 4. morning to night, 5. place to place/one place to another, 6. differ – each other.

15 1. eat it up, 2. get out, 3. hands off, 4. Look out, 5. carry on, 6. out with it

3.3 Wales and the Welsh

1 1. The differences between Wales and other parts of the British Isles are, firstly, that the Welsh have a much stronger national spirit and, secondly, that national traditions are much more important to them.
2. No, they haven't. It was seven hundred years ago when the two countries England and Wales became part of the same kingdom.
3. The Welsh, who are very musical, love singing songs, dancing traditional folk-dances and reciting poems.
4. North Wales attracts a lot of campers because of its campsites which are situated in beautiful countryside.
5. Many tourists want to spend their holidays at the seaside and therefore go to one of the many seaside resorts on the magnificent Welsh coast with its wonderful shores and bays.

6. The reason why the Welsh and the people from northern France can often understand each other is that the languages spoken in these countries have a lot in common.
7. The Welshman's remarks are much more polite than the Englishman's. It is very impolite to say that all Welshmen cannot be trusted, have a strange accent, make fun of others when speaking their impossible language and that even Scotsmen are more generous.

2 1. a competition which is held every year, 2. a lonely stretch of land, 3. beautiful landscape, 4. Both languages have much in common.

3 1. strength – power – force, 2. coast – shore – beach – banks, 3. country – county – ground/land – land – soil – nation

4 to succeed in, to apologize for, to appreciate, to continue, to hope, to mind, to insist on, to rely on, to enjoy, to manage, to object to, to refuse, to want, to like

5 1. gerund: to succeed in, to apologize for, to insist on, to rely on, to object to, to appreciate, to mind, to enjoy
2. infinitive: to hope, to manage, to refuse, to want
3. gerund or infinitive: to like, to continue

6 1. to speak, 2. speaking, 3. of doing, 4. at understanding, 5. to speaking, 6. on having, 7. on hearing, 8. to visit, 9. of going, 10. to be/being, 11. making, 12. to understand, 13. to see, 14. having seen, 15. going

7 1. You will enjoy your holidays (by) going to Wales. 2. By learning Welsh you will be able to understand a Breton. 3. You might understand something (by) listening attentively.

8 1. Welsh children have the chance of learning Welsh. 2. Why do they get the opportunity of learning this subject? 3. The English have no reason for speaking Welsh. 4. The Welsh insist on having their own TV programme. 5. John is proud of being Welsh. 6. The teacher blames Bob for not doing his homework. 7. People don't care for standing in queues. 8. You should listen to me instead of wasting your time. 9. They entered the room without knocking on the door. 10. He escaped from prison by jumping over the fence.

9 1. to, 2. of, 3. of, 4. at, 5. to

10 1. at, 2. of, 3. to, 4. of, 5. of

11 1. in, 2. in, 3. of, 4. in, 5. for

3.4 Indian Traditions in the West

1
1. Ranjana is 26 years old, she came to Britain eight years ago, so she was eighteen.
2. She will marry him because of her love for her parents who have arranged the marriage.
3. Ranjana is against arranged marriages. She believes that a girl should have the right to fall in love and marry the man of her own choice. She finds the idea of meeting her husband-to-be for the first time on her wedding day horrible.
4. a) If she agrees to the arranged marriage Ranjana is afraid of saying goodbye to all her freedom, especially as she got used to being away from home and enjoyed her independence.
   b) If she refuses the arranged marriage Ranjana is afraid of hurting her parents and bringing shame on the family. If she acted against Indian tradition by refusing the arranged marriage, this could upset and even break up the family unity.
5. The Indian tradition keeps families together in a way people do not have in the West.
6. When Ranjana says "It will not be a magnificent affair", she means that the marriage will not be a long ceremony and there will only be few guests.
7. No, she will not. If she has children, they will be free to choose their own partners.

2
1. Ranjana convinced her parents to consent to the meeting.
2. Things are at their worst when you understand that your marriage will definitely end your freedom.

3 1. Ranjana's marriage, planned by her parents, 2. the man whom she chooses by herself, 3. a school at which pupils are given lessons, meals and lodging, 4. a day on which a man and a woman become husband and wife, 5. they will be able to do as they like

4 1. She was trained at a boarding school. 2. He's a man she knows very little about. 3. I choose my husband on my own. 4. She saw her future husband. 5. I refuse arranged marriages. 6. I have discussed for a long time. 7. I'm accustomed to being away from home. 8. You know it's no use (or: it's hopeless). 9. I plan to write to him. 10. I know one thing for sure (or: I'm sure of one thing). 11. Perhaps I would meet someone.

5 1. wife, 2. headmistress, 3. bride, 4. widow, 5. actress, 6. heroine, 7. niece

6 1. intend, include, 2. receive, report, 3. inform, reform, insist, resist

7 1. might, 2. may, 3. may, 4. may/might, 5. might

8 1. He may come. 2. He may have arrived by now. 3. He may be working. 4. I may have been sleeping. 5. You may be right. 6. He may have lived in India. 7. He may have been waiting for us. 8. They may have been there.

9 1. may, 2. Can, 3. Can, 4. may – may not

10 1. was able, 2. has been able, 3. will be able, 4. was able, 5. will be able

11 1. needn't, 2. mustn't, 3. mustn't, 4. needn't, 5. mustn't, 6. needn't, 7. needn't

3.5 Levi's Blue Jeans

1 1. They went to California, because people had discovered gold (or: because gold had been discovered) there in 1848.
2. Selling jeans was much more profitable than finding gold.
3. No, there is not a big difference. The jeans have been sold almost unchanged for more than one hundred years.
4. His stepbrothers ran a shop selling needles, pins, scissors and cloth.
5. He planned to sell the miners rough canvas for their tents and wagon covers.
6. A gold seeker complained that their trousers did not wear for a long time, that they did not last, and that they wore badly.
7. Some of the miners were dissatisfied with the jeans, because the seams of the pockets were not strong enough.

Lösungen

2 1. clothes – cloth – clothing – tablecloths, 2. industrial – industrious, 3. business – shop – business – shops, 4. founded – founded – found, 5. fat – thick – fat, 6. immigrants – emigrants

3 1. dye – die, 2. take – bring – bring – bring, 3. carry – wear – carry, 4. role – roll – rolls, 5. price – prize – prizes – price

4

wealthy	wealth
original	origin
surprised	surprise
French	France
popular	popularity
fashionable	fashion

5 1. a thin cloth, 2. he immigrated, 3. they wear well (haltbar sein), 4. the same miners, 5. earlier

6 1. everything began with, 2. until/till now, 3. nearly unchanged, 4. with only one pair of trousers, 5. was the answer, 6. what they want/wish very much, 7. at the time of/during the Californian gold rush

7 born – far – death – left – become – found/discovered – become – seek/search for – sell – miners – self-made – dream – life – died

8 1. a needle, 2. a boss, 3. a tent, 4. to wear, 5. to complain, 6. to dye, 7. a sale

9

found	founded	founded	founding
find	found	found	finding
seek	sought	sought	seeking
die	died	died	dying
dye	dyed	dyed	dyeing
wear	wore	worn	wearing
spread	spread	spread	spreading

10 Once ashore, a gold seeker asked him what he had brought with him on that boat. Levi pointed to his rolls of strong cloth and said (that) he had brought those rolls of canvas there. The miner said (that) he should have brought trousers and that he should better sell trousers. The surprised newcomer asked why he (or: they) needed trousers there. The miner replied (that) their trousers wore out, (that) they didn't last, (that) they wore badly.

11 1. have sold, 2. make, 3. wore

12 1. "Are many trousers needed here?" 2. He was sent a thick cotton cloth from France.

13 1. "Hi, look at my new trousers, they are made of thick, strong cloth. I think they'll last for a long time. And they are comfortable as well."
2. "The seams of the pockets are not strong enough, they tear easily. Why don't they make them stronger?"
3. In the middle of the picture, there is a pair of trousers. There is one horse to the right and one to the left of these trousers, they are bound to the trousers with a rope. Two cowboys drive the horses, one to the right, the other to the left. Levi Strauss wanted to symbolize that his jeans are so strong that they cannot be torn even by horses.

14 Betty: Do you like my new trousers?
Sally: (...) Where did you buy them? (...) Were they very expensive?

15 1. Have you got yellow jeans? 2. My size is XL. 3. Where can I try them on? 4. I like them, but they are too wide. 5. Have you got smaller ones, one size smaller? 6. The smaller ones fit me. I'll take them.

16 1. I like it very much. 2. You look nice in your new dress/pullover. 3. It really suits you. 4. The colour goes well with your hair.

3.6 Coca-Cola

1 1. People buy 2,400,000 bottles of Coca-Cola per minute all over the world.
2. A pharmacist sells medicine.
3. Dr. Pemberton added a few coca bush leaves to the syrup.
4. They were astonished, because the Americans had Coca-Cola, too.
5. The expression is "world-famous refreshment".
6. You need change/coins which you put into the slot of the vending machine.

7. These prominent personalities are: sportsmen, film stars and presidents of the USA.
8. It is especially important, because millions of people all over the world watch the Olympic Games (or: The Olympic Games are broadcast in every corner of the world).
9. The economic system mentioned is capitalism.
10. The critics think that Coca-Cola is a symbol of the aggressive American politics. It shows the "Americanization" of the world.

2 1. to have a wrong idea, 2. the first and most important, 3. a person qualified to prepare and sell medicines, 4. to go on shore from a ship, 5. to have enough money for, 6. time free from work

3 1. factory, 2. Luxury, 3. magazine, 4. expert, 5. star

4 1. illness/disease, 2. slowly, 3. peace, 4. past, 5. far (away), 6. calmly, 7. friend/ally, 8. cheap, 9. hurry, 10. failure

5 1. to produce, 2. to explain, 3. to prove, 4. to succeed, 5. to advertise ['ædvətaɪz]

6 1. importance, 2. excitement, 3. poverty, 4. profit, 5. attraction, 6. aggression, 7. richness/riches, 8. difference

7 1. Dr. Pemberton, a pharmacist, was experimenting in his laboratory to find remedies for coughs, headaches, rheumatism or whatever could help people to restore their health.
2. Business with the soft drink grew rapidly, and it became the most important American product of the 20th century.
3. An officer asked for an explanation from a prisoner who spoke English.
4. Coke pays large sums for ads in newspapers, films, sports fields, and at car races.

8 1. hungry and thirsty, 2. medicines/remedies for most illnesses/diseases, 3. serve – waiter or waitress, 4. Soldiers – sailors, 5. money/profit by selling

9 1. invented, 2. discovered, 3. invented

10 1. story, 2. History, 3. story, 4. history

11 1. run, 2. travel, 3. drive

12 1. delicate, 2. delicate, 3. delicious

13 1. Coca-Cola managers are fond of telling this story to show (or: demonstrate) that there were no barriers.
2. Coke is kept cheap for underdeveloped countries which have not got much money (or: which cannot spend much money, or: which cannot pay a high price).
3. Coke's publicity experts have succeeded in winning prominent people.

14 1. on a one-armed bandit, 2. is an honest man, 3. wear a uniform, 4. me an umbrella, 5. that's a useful idea, 6. is a European country

15 1. is a car mechanic, 2. Is there (any) milk, 3. What terrible weather! 4. to become a stewardess, 5. What a terrible boy!

16 1. our guests' drinks, 2. the ladies' glasses, 3. the children's lemonades, 4. James's job, 5. today's paper, 6. my parents' (car), 7. at the chemist's

17 1. will get, 2. work, 3. would sell, 4. was, 5. had had

18 1. If she gave me her address, I could send her a birthday card.
2. If I had had enough money, I would have invited her for a drink.
3. If they had taken a taxi, they would not have arrived later.
4. If they had enough time, they would visit the museum.
5. If the weather had not been so bad, we would not have stayed in the hotel all the time.
6. If you take this medicine, you'll soon feel well again (or: If you took this medicine, you would soon feel well again).

19 1. if, 2. If, 3. when, 4. When

20 1. to – about, 2. of, 3. for – on – for – with – in – of

21 1. of, 2. for, 3. of, 4. for

22 1. How much is one bottle?
2. Where did you buy the drinks?
3. In which year/When was Coca-Cola invented?
4. At what time will we meet?
5. What does this drink smell of?

23 1. What would you like for dinner? – I'd like a soup first.
2. Do you prefer fish or meat? – I prefer fish.
3. Would you like something to drink? – Yes, a bottle/glass of mineral water, please.
4. How many kinds of cheese have they got? – They have got two kinds of cheese.
5. Did you tell the waiter to bring the bill? – Yes, I did.
6. This is quite a good restaurant, isn't it? – Indeed, it is.

24 1. I'll get/become too fat if I drink too much Coke.
2. If I had enough money, I would buy a bike.
3. If I had had more money, I would have bought more drinks for my birthday party.

4. Übersetzungen aus der Fremdsprache

4.1 Chistopher Kolumbus

Seit 1484 hatte Kolumbus versucht, die Herrscher von Portugal und Spanien zu überreden (oder: dazu zu bringen), sein Projekt (oder: Plan), einen neuen Seeweg (oder: Route) nach Indien zu finden, zu finanzieren. Schließlich erhielt (oder: gewann) Kolumbus die Unterstützung der spanischen Monarchen (oder: des spanischen Königspaares) Ferdinand und Isabella, und am 3. August 1492 begann die große Entdeckungsreise.

Wir wissen aus einer Kopie des Tagebuchs von Kolumbus, dass die Mannschaft unglücklich darüber war, in die endlose (oder: grenzenlose) See hinauszusegeln. Am 8. Oktober wollte die Besatzung (oder: Mannschaft) umkehren, aber Kolumbus sagte ihnen, sie sollten ihm den Kopf abschlagen und nach Europa zurückkehren, wenn sie nicht innerhalb von drei Tagen gelandet wären.

Als Kolumbus und seine Männer endlich die Karibischen Inseln erreichten, begann die Suche nach Gold und Edelsteinen. 32 Wochen später kehrte Kolumbus heim, ohne dass er auch nur einen einzigen Mann auf See verloren hätte (oder: ohne einen einzigen Mann auf See verloren zu haben). Obwohl (es) einige Leute abstritten, dass Kolumbus bis nach Indien gekommen sei, wurde er an den spanischen Hof eingeladen, wo er mit großen Ehren empfangen wurde.

Auf seiner zweiten Reise (oder: Seereise) nahm Kolumbus 17 Schiffe, 1.500 Seeleute, Soldaten und Siedler mit. An Bord hatten sie auch

Pflanzen, Tiere und Werkzeuge für eine dauerhafte (oder: beständige) Ansiedelung.

4.2 Einwanderung heute

Jede Woche kommen 2.500 Einwanderer auf dem J. F. Kennedy-Flughafen an. Diese Einwanderer kommen aus den gleichen Gründen, die die Menschen in der Vergangenheit in die Vereinigten Staaten geführt haben: Sie wollen der Unterdrückung entkommen und ein besseres Leben für sich selbst und ihre Kinder finden. Aber heute kommen sie aus anderen Teilen der Welt.
Während bis 1950 die Mehrzahl der Einwanderer aus Europa kam, kommen die heutigen Auswanderer aus Asien, der Karibik und aus Lateinamerika. Die neuen Amerikaner bekommen eine so genannte „Greencard". Diese Karte ist eine Arbeitsgenehmigung und berechtigt sie, auf Dauer in den Staaten zu wohnen.
Natürlich reisen viele Einwanderer ohne Erlaubnis ein. Roberto zum Beispiel. Ich lernte ihn in New York kennen. Er trug an einem kalten Nachmittag im Januar einen dünnen Pullover und verkaufte mexikanische Süßigkeiten, womit er 35 Dollar am Tag verdiente. In Mexico City war er Automechaniker gewesen, aber in New York konnte er ohne Greencard nur Arbeit als Verkäufer finden.
Ein „Reisevermittler" hatte ihn nachts über die Grenze geführt und in ein Flugzeug nach New York verfrachtet – für 700 Dollar, die Roberto sich von einem Verwandten geliehen hatte.
Der Kongress versucht, solch illegaler Einwanderung ein Ende zu machen. Es wurde ein Gesetz erlassen, welches Arbeitgeber bestraft, die Arbeiter ohne Papiere einstellen. Dennoch kommen illegale Einwanderer auch weiterhin, wie Roberto, der mir erzählte: „Ich mag Amerika. Ich verdiene Geld und ich fühle mich wohl hier."

4.3 Was der National Trust für Sie bereithält

Wenn Sie glauben, dass es dem National Trust hauptsächlich um Landhäuser und ihre Inhalte geht, dann haben Sie nur zum Teil Recht. Denn neben seinen 250 historischen Gebäuden schützt der Trust – für uns alle und für alle Zeiten – auch Gärten und landschaftlich gestaltete Parks, Landschaft, darunter Wälder und baumloses Hügelland, Seen, Berge und die Hälfte unserer herrlichsten verbliebenen Küste, prähistorische und römische Stätten, Überreste unserer industriellen Ver-

gangenheit, mehr als tausend Bauernhöfe – sogar vierzig urtümliche Dörfer. Rechnen Sie zu diesen seine 165 Geschäfte hinzu, seine einladenden Restaurants mit lokalen Gerichten, seine Landschaftsparks, Naturschutzgebiete und seine Ferienhäuschen und Sommerfestspiele, und wir können ansatzweise den Reichtum des britischen Erbes, das der National Trust besitzt, ermessen.
All dies zu unterhalten kostet mehr als 50 Millionen Pfund im Jahr. Aber der Trust ist keineswegs eine Regierungsstelle. Da er keine regelmäßigen öffentlichen Gelder erhält, wird er durch den Privatsektor am Leben erhalten – durch gewöhnliche Leute wie Sie und ich. Wenn Sie helfen wollen, ist es am besten, wenn Sie dem Trust beitreten.
Die Häuser des National Trust bieten Spaß und Faszination für alle und sorgen nicht nur dafür, dass sich Ihre Mitgliedschaft auszahlt, sondern sie lassen Sie auch erkennen, wie wir Mitgliedsbeiträge verwenden. Was für eine Freizeitbeschäftigung Sie auch immer wählen, der National Trust hat Ihnen etwas anzubieten.

4.4 Rasenmäher, die kein Gras mähen

Es ist ein regnerischer Samstagmorgen in einem Vorort von Sheffield. Ein Herr mittleren Alters versucht, trotz des Regens einen Rasenmäher in Gang zu setzen. Immer wieder zieht er am Seil, und schließlich gelingt es ihm, den Motor der Maschine anzuwerfen. Der Herr setzt seinen Sturzhelm auf, schwingt sich in den Sitz und röhrt davon.
Er fährt zu einer nicht weit von seinem Reihenhaus entfernten großen Weide. Ungefähr sechzig Fahrer mit dröhnenden Motoren warten auf ihn. Sie sind umgeben von Rauchwolken und ohrenbetäubendem Lärm.
Um neun Uhr beginnt das Rasenmäherrennen. Es ist ein Ausdauerrennen, das zwölf Stunden dauert. Bei diesem Rennen wird kein einziger Grashalm geschnitten, da die Messer der Rasenmäher aus Sicherheitsgründen entfernt werden.
Entlang der Rennstrecke herrscht eine Atmosphäre wie auf einem Campingplatz: Wohnwagen und Zelte, Würstchen- und Eiscremestände, lärmende Kinder, die im Matsch herumlaufen, Mütter, die im Freien unter großen Schirmen das schmutzige Geschirr abwaschen, Väter, die auf Liegestühlen liegen und Hunde, die an Grills herumschnüffeln.

Das Rennen wird organisiert von der BLMRA, der British Lawn Mower Racing Association, dem Britischen Rasenmäherrennverband, der von Britain's Royal Automobile Club, dem Königlichen Automobilclub-Großbritanniens, anerkannt ist. Es findet fast jedes Wochenende auf dem Feld irgendeines Landwirts statt.
Natürlich hat die BLMRA strenge Regeln. Drei eng bedruckte Seiten schreiben alles genauestens vor, von der Form des Sitzes bis zur Anzahl der Boxenstopps. Die wichtigste Regel ist, dass die Mäher zum Mähen von privaten Rasenflächen und nicht etwa von Golfplätzen oder öffentlichen Grünanlagen hergestellt und verkauft worden sein müssen.
Ein BBC-Reporter stellte während einer Fernsehübertragung des 12-Stunden-Ausdauerrennens fest: „Dies ist ein klassischer britischer Sport: betrieben von Fanatikern, mit absurden Regeln und meistens im Regen."